PRAISE FOR JEFF SHORE AND
FOLLOW UP AND CLOSE THE SALE

No. It's a word that every salesperson hears, often several times a day. In *Follow Up and Close the Sale*, Jeff Shore teaches you what to do next—in particular, how to develop the mindset of serving your customers by following up. Shore's treatment of this topic, which has frustrated sales professionals for decades, is long overdue and exceedingly wise.

—Daniel H. Pink, #1 *New York Times* bestselling
author of *To Sell Is Human*

This powerful, practical, fast-moving book is loaded with proven strategies and techniques that you can use to make more and bigger sales, faster and easier than ever before.

—Brian Tracy, bestselling author of *The Psychology of Selling*

Jeff Shore is the master of follow-up, and he will teach you how to close more sales and make more money using this powerful tool. In this book, you will learn more and better ways to follow up than you dreamed possible. I recommend it.

—Mark Sanborn, bestselling author of *The Potential Principle*
and *The Intention Imperative*

Jeff Shore has done it again! In a simple-to-implement format, he has managed to powerfully and effectively teach the missing link to championship sales success. If you are a sales professional, read this book and begin applying its message right away.

—Bob Burg, bestselling coauthor of *The Go-Giver*
and author of *Endless Referrals*

What separates winners from losers when it comes to winning big deals is their disciplined follow-up and follow-through, being persistent, and proving they are reliable. Read this book, improve your effectiveness, and win more deals.

—Anthony Iannarino, author of *Eat Their Lunch*

Jeff has written one of the strongest books on sales I have come across in a long time. Power-packed with strategies, loaded with information, and writing that keeps you glued to the content. Read this book, share this book, and use this book to land more deals.

—Meridith Elliott Powell, CEO of MotionFirst

Jeff has provided the solution to the big problem everyone faces. You don't just read this book, you make money from this book! Read it now—before your competitor does.

—Mark Hunter ("The Sales Hunter"), author of
The Mind for Sales and *High-Profit Prospecting*

Jeff Shore is one of the strongest voices in sales. He speaks with power and wisdom, and the truths and tips in *Follow Up and Close the Sale* will increase your confidence, your effectiveness, your win rate, and your paycheck!

—Mike Weinberg, bestselling author of *New Sales. Simplified.*

Pay attention to the brilliant methodology in this valuable book. Jeff's strategic vision and practical advice provide every sales professional with the process and tools needed to accelerate follow-up strategies, stand out, and get the attention and results you want and need. If you are a sales leader, read this book and buy a copy for everyone in your team. You'll be so glad you did.

—Neen James, author of *Attention Pays*

In sports, the ball goes where you want it to go, because of how you follow through. The same is true for sales. Finally, a book that addresses the weakest part of most sales processes! Bravo, Jeff Shore!

—Bill Cates, president of Referral Coach International

Sales nurturing and follow-up are a mix of art, skills, and psychology. Anyone who receives an endless barrage of "just checking in" emails or calls, or the infamous "were you abducted by aliens" email, can relate to follow-up being done poorly. What's even worse is no follow-up at all. What we don't see enough is consistent follow-up, done well. Jeff Shore has a formula and proven system for helping you fix that and excel at follow-up, in a way that is customer-centric, engages buyers, and gets results. If you follow Jeff's work already, that's no surprise. If you don't yet, jump in. You'll be glad you did.

—Mike Kunkle, VP at Sales Enablement Services

Here's the deal. If you follow up with buyers, you will win more sales. As a bonus, you build your brand as a salesperson who is truly committed to your clients' best outcome. Jeff provides the mindsets and the techniques for selling more while making it easy and fun.

—Dr. John Musser, founder and CEO of Enhanced Sales Potential

The key to any sale is effective follow-up, yet most sales executives, including top performers, do not do this effectively on a consistent basis, and are leaving huge amounts of money on the table. If you want to close more sales, read this book!

—Ron Karr, creator of the Velocity Mindset™ and
author of *Lead, Sell, or Get Out of the Way*

As someone who believes follow-up is one of the top keys to success in sales, it is so refreshing to read Jeff Shore's simple way of teaching the fundamentals. By focusing on mindset, strategy, and then execution, he takes a process many of us don't do well and breaks it down into tactical, executable steps. Bravo!

—Lori Richardson, CEO of Score More Sales

From time to time a book comes along that can make a difference. Jeff Shore's new work is a striking example. Jeff provides a comprehensive and engaging exploration of the fundamentally important topic of follow-up, and shares the best practices and tools required to overcome our resistance to the task.

—Richard Ruff, PhD, partner at Level Five Selling

This isn't just a collection of follow-up tactics. It's a sales relationship manifesto. Make this required reading for anyone you trust to sell for you. It turns the agony of follow-up into purposeful excitement.

—Tim David, author of *Magic Words* and
The Four Levels of Influencing People

This book is guaranteed to change how you think about follow-up. With his signature use of stories and sales humor, Jeff Shore uncovers the truth about why most follow-up fails, and how you can use the follow-up secrets of sales legends to unleash a new level of success.

—Dennis O'Neil, president of ONeil Interactive Inc.

Another winning book from Jeff Shore to add to your sales arsenal. Jeff's approach to the mindset and execution of the sales process is second to none.

—Scott Lalli, president of Destination Homes

This straightforward approach to customer follow-up offers techniques that are easy to use and easy to understand. Jeff has a proven track record and his insight into this topic is spot on.

—Doug Moran, COO of Dream Finders Homes

Another great work by Jeff! He is always on point with current sales needs, and this book is no exception. His witty and easy-to-read style conveys real actionable advice to sales professionals in all industries. A must-read for the sales superstar!

—Wade Thomas, founder and CEO of Aim to Win

Jeff Shore hits upon a critical component of the sales process to which most salespeople pay little mind. In *Follow Up and Close the Sale*, he provides key strategies and techniques to keep the sale moving and help you win more deals at the prices you want. Your follow-up methods differentiate you and can provide value the competition does not. Take advantage of those opportunities to set yourself apart.

—Lee B. Salz, author of *Sales Differentiation*

FOLLOW UP
AND CLOSE

MAKE EASY (AND EFFECTIVE)
FOLLOW-UP YOUR WINNING HABIT

THE

SALE

FOLLOW UP
AND CLOSE
MAKE EASY (AND EFFECTIVE) FOLLOW-UP YOUR WINNING HABIT
THE SALE

JEFF SHORE

New York   Chicago   San Francisco   Athens   London   Madrid
Mexico City   Milan   New Delhi   Singapore   Sydney   Toronto

2 3 4 5 6 7 8 9   LCR   25 24 23 22 21 20

ISBN: 978-1-260-46266-1
MHID: 1-260-46266-8

e-ISBN: 978-1-260-46267-8
e-MHID: 1-260-46267-6

Library of Congress Cataloging-in-Publication Data

Names: Shore, Jeff, author.
Title: Follow up and close the sale / Jeff Shore.
Description: New York : McGraw-Hill, [2020] | Includes bibliographical
    references and index.
Identifiers: LCCN 2020005686 (print) | LCCN 2020005687 (ebook) | ISBN
    9781260462661 (hardcover) | ISBN 9781260462678 (ebook)
Subjects: LCSH: Selling.
Classification: LCC HF5438.25 .S5626 2020 (print) | LCC HF5438.25 (ebook) |
    DDC 658.85—dc23
LC record available at https://lccn.loc.gov/2020005686
LC ebook record available at https://lccn.loc.gov/2020005687

McGraw-Hill Education books are available at special quantity discounts to use as premiums and sales promotions or for use in corporate training programs. To contact a representative, please visit the Contact Us pages at www.mhprofessional.com.

To the incredibly talented team at Shore Consulting.
You are both friends and family. Your passion and dedication
inspire me each and every day. I love you all.

Contents

PART III
EXECUTION

PART IV
KILLIN' IT

Foreword

Salespeople Don't Follow Up

At a trade show earlier this year I met a sales representative who was working her company's booth. We had a great conversation, and once I learned more about her service, I was ready to buy. In fact, I said those words. So, I gave her my email and direct mobile number and asked her to call me on Monday. She didn't. In fact, she never followed up.

This past spring, we were helping an elderly (and quite wealthy) relative with finding an upscale, full-service retirement facility. We visited seven facilities, did tours, and listened to their sales presentations. All of the salespeople seemed eager to work with us. They all had empty beds to fill. Only one ever followed up, and even then, his single email was tepid, passive, and lame.

Three weeks ago, I was shopping for insurance for my growing company. I did discovery calls with several agents. All of them promised to follow up with quotes. Only one did.

The sad truth is that salespeople don't follow up, and honestly, I don't know why. The money is on the table just waiting for someone to pick it up! Ineffective and nonexistent sales follow-up is a gaping hole in the sales profession. The brutal truth is that 44 percent of salespeople give up after *only* one follow-up attempt.

The irony is that, oftentimes, the sales professionals who claim to be desperate for better results are the same ones who neglect this important discipline. In a world that offers a never-ending smorgasbord of shortcuts and get-rich-quick schemes, we tend to ignore what is perhaps the most important success trait of all: *perseverance*.

Ultra-high-performing salespeople will tell you that the one trait that sets them apart from everyone else is the discipline to persevere. I work with top-tier sales professionals each day from every corner of the globe who tell stories of calling and calling and calling until finally breaking through and scoring their dream account. One of the largest deals I ever sold was closed after leaving 52 voice mails. Because that's what it took!

But if you consider the examples I opened with, we're not even talking about perseverance. We're talking about common sense. We're talking about leaving easy money on the table. Those reps were too afraid or too undisciplined to just pick up the phone and follow up. The truth is it takes discipline, commitment, getting past your fear of objections, a willingness to work through resistance, and a desire to win in order to master sales follow-up.

Jeff Shore has a message for you: If you wish to stand out from your competition, be a hero in your organization, and find unparalleled success, follow-up is the path that will get you there. In *Follow Up and Close the Sale* Jeff teaches you exactly what you need to do to put more money in your pocket now! If you're ready to take your sales career to the next level, turn the page and get to work.

Jeb Blount
Founder and CEO of Sales Gravy and author
of 12 books, including *Fanatical Prospecting,
Sales EQ, People Buy You, Objections,* and *INKED*

Acknowledgments

Billy Joel wrote the soundtrack to my youth. I'm a big fan, and I've seen him in concert many times over the years. Last year my wife and I saw him perform at Madison Square Garden in New York City. Our seats were to the side of the stage, and this gave us an interesting angle to see some of what was happening behind the scenes. It was a Billy Joel concert, and his name was written in huge letters, but hundreds of people helped to make the concert a success.

So too with writing a book. The reader doesn't get to see the toil, the arguments, the research, the editing, and all the other painstaking tasks that go into the process.

But I do. I observe firsthand the amount of work that goes into putting a book together, and the effort is Herculean.

For one thing, everyone on the Shore Consulting team plays a part in the process. Paul Murphy constructs the promo videos and pushes the book on various channels. Kelly King works with our clients on the "friends and family" book promotions. Bevin Curtis handles the keynote speaking requests that always come in when a book is released. Cassandra Grauer coordinates book launch events. Amy O'Connor and Ryan Taft contribute invaluable content notes and also teach the content to thousands upon thousands of sales professionals each year. Kevin Shore manages the "backstage" portion of the book, including listings, shipping and fulfillment, and online campaigns. Ali Westbrook leads the digital marketing and social media team. And Wade Mayhue oversees the project as a de facto executive producer.

But then there is the really heavy lifting. Nancy Bach was an invaluable resource, both as a researcher and as a first-rate line editor. Nancy's job was to make me look good (or, more accurately, to minimize the occurrences of my looking stupid). And Laura Smith managed this entire project. Laura played several roles: taskmaster, encourager, file manager, production supervisor, format expert, and more. You cannot see them with the naked eye, but Laura's fingerprints are all over this book.

Thanks as well to Casey Ebro, executive editor at McGraw Hill, and to the entire McGraw Hill team. Thank you for your belief, for your patience, and for your dedication to excellence. Likewise, huge props to my agent, Sheree Bykofsky. Your blend of dogged determination and a tell-it-like-it-is style is just what this author needs to stay on track.

Big thanks to the frontline sales professionals who contributed to this book: Carla Adal, Jason Burrows, Greg Cook, Desiree Elderkin, Elisa Estock, Darla Hartline, Cheryl Holthaus, Paul Hurme, Molly Jacobs, Krystal Land, Kelly Lopez, Monika Newman, Austin Oswinkle, Peter Papadopoulos, Lynn Rafuse, Randy Ratkowski, Scott Roulier, Steve Ruggiero, Annette Schavietello, Vince Sciarrabba, Nancy Shaw, Tim Sweat, Stephen Turner, Summer Williams, Joe Wobeter, and many others.

Much appreciation to the sales gurus who contributed: Matt Heinz, Anthony Iannarino, Mike Kunkle, Alen Mayer, Todd Reynolds, Richard Ruff, Elinor Stutz, and Viveka von Rosen.

Finally, thanks to my wife, Karen. She had the unenviable task of watching me grind through the writing of the book. She bore the brunt of my emotional turmoil throughout the process. And she will share the joy when the book goes to number one on the new releases chart (well, here's hoping!). Love you, baby.

And finally, finally, I am blessed to hear so much positive feedback from the thousands of sales professionals I have had the wonderful opportunity to teach and lead over the years. Your warm comments never get old. Thank you for trusting me to help with your ongoing success.

s. D. g.*

---

* Bach wrote the initials s.D.g. at the bottom of each of his musical pieces. From the Latin "Soli Deo Gloria"—to God Alone. It's a signature I have adopted.

Introduction

We perform at our highest level when we serve others. We perform at our lowest level when we serve only ourselves.

The scene: the climax of your sales presentation.

You prepare to ask boldly and confidently for the sale, fully expecting a yes. You've already calculated your commission. OK, fine—you've already *spent* the commission. You deliver the world's most perfect close. Zig Ziglar himself would have been proud.

Then the unthinkable happens.

"No? What do you mean, no? You had a problem and I solved it. This is perfect for you. It's everything any customer would ever want, and at great terms. And now you want to 'think about it'? Think about *what*? I just gave you the best pitch I've got!"

Arghhh!

At this point you think to yourself, "Oh, well. You can't win 'em all, right? Perhaps I can sell to the next person who walks through the door."

What? Hold the phone. *You ain't done yet!*

THE PROBLEM

For too many salespeople, the process ends when the customer says no. Theirs is a strategy of hope. As in, "I hope they come back because, if I'm being honest, I'll never call them again. Yeah, maybe an email in a week or so, but if they're really interested, they'll let me know sooner."

What? You did all that fine work throughout the entire presentation, and now you're going to just quit? That's like running a marathon and sitting down in a coffee shop with a half mile left to go.

In other words, that's a waste. Worse, it is a tremendous disservice to your customer. Worse than even that, a lack of follow-up is just plain rude. And yet a complete lack of follow-up is the norm for far too many sales practitioners.

This stark and all-too-common reality is actually *good* news for those sales professionals who understand that sales follow-up not only is great for the pocketbook but is also an invaluable part of the service they provide to a customer.

These sales stars are winners, the ones who go above and beyond to stay with their customers until their problems have been solved, no matter what it takes. They are the grinders, the persistent ones, the people who know that nuggets of pure gold are just waiting in the follow-up mines. They just have to dig a little bit.

Maybe you're in the first group, those salespeople who are waiting for customers to purchase on their first visit—and if the customer doesn't purchase on visit one, then waiting for the customer to take the initiative and make the next move.

Maybe you're in the second group, the ones who know no limits when it comes to doing everything it takes to keep the sale moving forward. The doggedly persistent, the intensely creative, the opposite of quitters. "No" is just another way for a customer to say "not yet."

Chances are you're probably somewhere in the middle. You are doing some follow-up, but you know you could improve. Your CRM is underutilized. Your efforts are rote and automatic. It's not fun for you, and you suspect that your customer finds no great joy nor any particular benefit from your communications.

If that description is accurate, then this book is for you.

THE SOLUTION

You're busy. You lack both time and energy. You know there is more to do in the area of follow-up, but adopting some kind of massive and intricate system that requires you to pound the phone for hours on end holds absolutely zero appeal.

I'm with you. I am all about finding methods and techniques that are simple, easy to understand, and, dare I say, even enjoyable.

If you're looking to seriously improve your follow-up game without having to reinvent your entire approach, read on. By the time you're finished, you will find:

- Simplicity—an approach to follow-up that is customer-centric and exceedingly easy to track

- Confidence—a winning mindset that's motivated by doing the right thing: for yourself, for your company, and mostly for your customer

- Sales success—a way to shorten the buying cycle and net more sales

MY JOURNEY

I'll start with a confession. Sales follow-up did not come easy to me. I am a face-to-face guy with some telephobia issues. (I'll address that unfortunate condition in Chapter 10.) Follow-up was something I did because my sales manager made me do it. Basically, I went through the motions.

Here's the problem: I was still making sales. I was still effective because of my visit-one closing skills. I didn't *need* to rely on follow-up.

And then it all came tumbling down. I was selling real estate, and the market crumbled around me. The visit-one sales went away. Suddenly, I was forced to rely on follow-up skills that I simply did not possess.

That was the beginning of my journey to becoming a complete salesperson. That's right—complete. If you are in sales and you have not perfected the art of follow-up, you are incomplete. Period. You have a gaping hole in your game, which will haunt you sooner or later.

That was a turnaround point for my sales career. Now 30-plus years later I have coached tens of thousands of sales professionals on all aspects of the sales process.

But I approach sales in a different way.

I am extremely interested in the way that salespeople sell, but I am far more interested in the way that buyers buy. My philosophy: If we understand the way people make purchase decisions, we can reverse engineer our sales presentation to make it easy for them to do just that.

Basically, I invite you to sell the way a buyer wants to buy. That mental approach will make all the difference between mediocre follow-up and stellar follow-through.

THE QUICK TOUR

For this book, I have a macro-to-micro approach. I'll start with the big picture and then drill down into the follow-up weeds.

Part I deals with mindset. I'll talk about what separates the winners from the losers. I will highlight some sales follow-up superstars, and I'll address what Steven Pressfield calls Resistance. (I often find that Resistance is really just a comfort addiction.)

The most important objective is to get you to fall in love with follow-up. That's right, I want you to not simply endure follow-up, but to actually look forward to it. That's the fun part!

Part II is all about strategy. This begins with understanding customers' buying mindsets, how they make purchase decisions, and how they utilize decision-making shortcuts.

From there we will identify what I call the sales superpowers—there are two—that will allow you to stand apart from the competition quickly and effectively.

Part III focuses on execution. This is the nuts-and-bolts part of the book. This is about crafting the perfect follow-up contact, be it by phone, text, email, note, or any other medium you choose. We'll talk about developing a system that you can adhere to every single day.

Part III is where you shine. It's where you shorten that buying cycle. Part III is where the winners hang out.

Part IV is aimed at getting you ready to soar to heights you have never before experienced. This section is about joining the top 1 percent of sales professionals around the world.

HOW TO USE THIS BOOK

I encourage you to do two things.

First, read the book from front to back. I've written nine books, and many of them allow the reader to jump around to find a specific solution to a specific problem. This book is not like that. You really want to let the concepts unfold a little at a time.

Think of this book as the structural elements of a house. The Mindset section is the foundation. The Strategy section symbolizes the walls. The Execution section is the roof. If you skip any of those elements, you end up with a weak and silly-looking house.

Second, read actively. Read with a pen in your hand. Write in the margins. Ask questions of yourself and of the text. Challenge everything.

This book is designed to enable you to craft your own personalized solution based on what you learn and discover along the way.

WHAT THIS BOOK IS NOT

This is not an alternative to your CRM. Most every organization I work with already has a follow-up system in place, along with thorough CRM software. This book is meant to complement such systems and processes. The ideas are adaptable to any existing system.

This is not a one-size-fits-all. Every organization is different, and the number of defined sales processes are endless. Take the concepts and principles herein and apply them to your current programs. It would be foolish to suggest that you throw out what works and start over again.

There are segments in this book that won't work for you. On the whole, I believe that every sales professional will find value in the pages that follow. But I can guarantee that you will come across strategies that simply do not apply to your specific situation. For example, I write for a largely business-to-consumer audience. While I am certain that business-to-business sales professionals will benefit greatly from the advice in this book, they may need to customize this to scenarios that involve large-scale enterprise-level sales.

MY PROMISE TO YOU

I teach the way I like to be taught . . . and I have a very short attention span.

I'll keep the chapters short and to the point. I'll tell stories to illustrate concepts. They will always be actual case studies from real salespeople. I won't embellish, I won't make up statistics, and I won't suggest techniques you won't use.

I will honor sales as the noble profession that it is. And I will honor you as the one who is blessed with an incredible opportunity each day—the chance to impact someone's life.

FOLLOW UP
AND CLOSE
MAKE EASY (AND EFFECTIVE)
FOLLOW-UP YOUR WINNING HABIT
THE
SALE

PART I
MINDSET

1

The *Why* of Follow-Up

*Effective follow-up is relationship based
and service driven. This is not about you;
it is about serving the people you love.*

SHOW THAT YOU CARE

Quick question: Do you care about the people closest to you in your life?
Of course you do. You're a stellar human being, right?

Follow-up question: How do those people *know* that you care? What
is the evidence of your caring attitude? And before you say it, that subscription to the sock-of-the-month club you gave them for Christmas does
not count.

We prove our care by how we serve.

Martin Luther King Jr. once said, "Life's most persistent and urgent
question is: What are you doing for others?" Agreed. It's not just important—it's urgent.

Whether to your spouse, your kids, your friends, your coworkers, or
anyone else in your life, you show your concern and compassion by your
level of service. In other words, caring is an action, not an attitude.

One final question: Do you care about your customers?

Don't answer yet. In fact, don't answer at all. *Show me; don't tell me.*

Show me how you serve your customer, and I'll see just how much
you care.

> ### FROM THE FIELD
>
> Does caring matter? Yes! "With phone follow-up I was told by a customer, 'We were going to buy with whoever called us first out of you three.' They told me one rep texted, another sent an email, but I was the only one to actually call and check in to make sure they made it back home safely. They said, 'We wanted to buy from someone who we knew cared about us, and not just the sale.' They signed a contract with me the next day."

WHY YOU SHOULD FOLLOW UP

There are plenty of reasons to follow up with a customer:

- Because it's part of your job and you'll get in trouble if you fail to make the calls.
- Because you owe the customer an answer on something.
- Because you'll feel guilty if you don't.
- Because you really need the sale.

All these reasons are legitimate, but they all fall far short of the real reason to follow up: to serve the customer.

> ### FROM THE FIELD
>
> My company, Shore Consulting, surveyed hundreds of salespeople in the field for this book. Nearly all said follow-up was important to their success, with 82 percent reporting it was *crucially* important.

Suppose you are single and hoping to find that someone special. You are invited to a wedding, and at the reception you strike up a conversation with a friend of a friend. You hit it off extremely well. In fact, for the next three hours you spend the entire time with that person. There is a deep connection, a spark, if you will. You give that person your contact information, and in exchange you receive the promise of a phone call very soon.

And then you never hear from that person again. (Wah-wah . . . sad trombone.)

What are you to think—that the person you were talking with didn't care? Actually, it's worse than that. You are left to believe that the individual *never* cared, that it was all a charade, that this person was, in effect, faking it.

Is it any different with customers? You spend time together, you share important details, and you develop a strong, trust-based rapport.

And then the customers never hear from you again. Or if they do hear from you, it's a formulaic email that only proves that they weren't worth so much as a personalized note, let alone a phone call.

As you can see, there is a lot at stake here. If you truly care about your customers, prove it. Prove it in your follow-up.

> *Not following up with your prospects is the same as filling up your bathtub without first putting the stopper in the drain.*
>
> —MICHELLE MOORE

CASE STUDY

At a conference recently I was pitched an intriguing business idea by someone who wanted to ghostwrite the very book you are reading right now.

Her opening was outstanding: "Jeff, what do you have more of—time or money?"

Now, I'm not saying I'm rich by any stretch, but that question was easy to answer. Time is always in exceedingly short supply, and I told her so.

Then came the close: "Give us a shot to write the book for you. You'll exchange money, which you have, for time, which you need."

I'm not going to lie. It was a good line, and I was definitely intrigued.

Let's unpack that story.

At Shore Consulting we teach our clients The Buying Formula,™ a formula for how people make purchase decisions. People buy when:

$$Current\ Dissatisfaction \times Future\ Promise > Cost + Fear$$
$$(CD \times FP > C + F)$$

When customers are highly dissatisfied with their current situation (CD), and they see a tremendous amount of promise in your solution (FP), they are more inclined to overcome their fear-based doubts, accept the cost, and pay the price, both financial and mental (C + F).

With that formula in mind, go back to the ghostwriter who pitched me and consider this question: How high was my Current Dissatisfaction *before* our conversation?

The fact is that I had no dissatisfaction. I had written a number of books on my own and hardly felt that I needed help in that process (see figure). But the conversation raised my CD; I had to admit that I am continually frustrated by my lack of available time.

Comparing Levels of Dissatisfaction

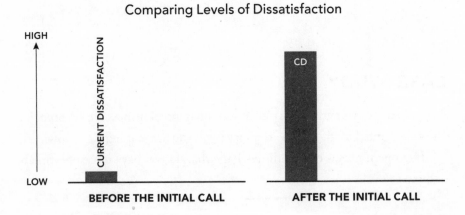

Next question: How high was my Future Promise *before* our conversation?

Again, it was very low (see figure). I did not understand the process, and I didn't see how someone could effectively capture my voice through ghostwriting. But the sales conversation raised my confidence in her ability to create a great product with a minimal investment of my time.

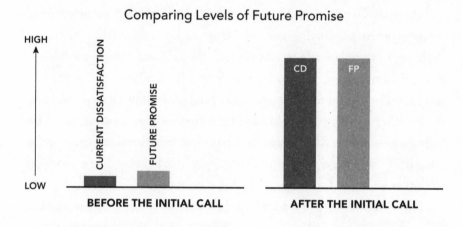

Finally, how high was my Cost + Fear *before* the sales conversation? It was sky high, insurmountable even (see figure). My C + F was based upon a raging fear of the unknown. But I was intrigued enough to watch that factor slip down the scale just a bit.

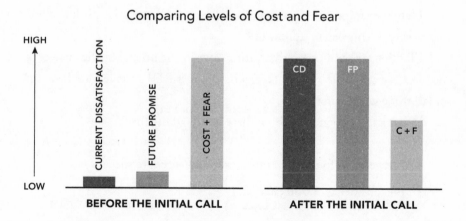

Your Customer's Emotional Altitude

What I have described in the story thus far is a critical aspect of the buying journey, an aspect that informs the very *why* of follow-up. I call this *Emotional Altitude*. I'll dive into the importance of emotion in the purchase process in Chapter 2, but for now, just know that in the absence of emotion you simply will not get a sale. Period.

The Emotional Altitude represents the level of the two motivating components in The Buying Formula: Current Dissatisfaction and Future Promise. In short, people buy when both the CD and the FP are high—and they won't buy when those factors are low. But understand that the CD and FP are both emotional elements; they trigger feelings deep in our core.

In other words, people do not begin their buying journey based on their dissatisfaction. They begin based on their emotional response to the dissatisfaction. Likewise, people do not purchase because of the promise, but rather because of the emotion tied to the promise.

Now back to the story. I told the salesperson/writer that I wanted to discuss her proposal with my team and mull it over. I was excited about the possibility, but I had some work to do. She offered to jump on the phone with anyone on my team—good strategy!—but I politely declined. Conversation over.

We pause now for reflection on how critical the next action is. If you miss this, you'll miss the point of the entire book.

Here's an important question for you, oh brilliant sales philosopher: *When* should this person follow up?

I'll offer my opinion on the timing later in the book, but the answer is not *in three weeks*. That is, in fact, what happened. I received a follow-up email three weeks later.

What had happened in those three weeks of my life?

- I traveled to four different states giving keynote speeches.

- I received over 3,000 emails.

- I made or received several hundred phone calls.
- I went to Hawaii on vacation.
- I forgot all about anything related to work for 11 days.
- I came home to more emails than I could possibly count.
- I wore out the delete key on my computer.

So here it is, three weeks later, the follow-up email. Where is my Emotional Altitude by this time? It's so low that it doesn't even register on the scale.

Get the picture? This salesperson was back at square one, starting all over again with a customer who had a thousand other things on his mind.

You might think that this is a story about speed. It's not.

It's a story of respect, or lack thereof.

> *Great salespeople are relationship builders who provide value and help their customers win.*
>
> —JEFFREY GITOMER

THE CORE MINDSET

Let me put it another way. If you want to get your head on straight when it comes to follow-up, you need to remember two factors.

Follow-up must be:

1. Relationship based
2. Service driven

Your follow-up should be an extension of the trust relationship that you have already established. And you should approach follow-up with one goal in mind: *to serve your customer.*

THE BAD NEWS

The numbers don't lie, people. Here is the sad reality:

- 44 percent of salespeople give up after one follow-up attempt.[1]
- The average sales rep makes only two attempts to reconnect with a prospect.[2]
- 42 percent of sales reps feel they don't have enough information to make a follow-up call.[3]
- 80 percent of calls go to voice mail, and 90 percent of first-time voice mails are never returned.[4]
- 85 percent of prospects and customers are dissatisfied with their on-the-phone experience.[5]

It's bad news . . . for most folks. But very good news for those who recognize the opportunity. My friend, you can stand out like a show dog in a kennel if you do this right. This is low-hanging fruit, and it is yours for the pickin'. Reach out and grab it!

THE MYTHS

You might have been guilty in the past of a mental dialogue that sounds like this:

- "I'd rather spend my time on new leads."
- "I already heard a no, so the show's over."
- "I don't want to annoy people."

I would simply ask you this question: How successful do you want to be? Because the stories you've been telling yourself about follow-up are standing in the way of reaching your sales potential.

Look, I'm not going to sit behind my computer and tell you that you will land a sale on 100 percent of your follow-up calls. Or 50 percent. Or 25 percent. The fact is, I don't know the number . . . and neither do you, until you give it your best effort.

In many ways, follow-up is like marketing. They say that only 10 percent of all marketing is effective, and the problem is that we never know which 10 percent it is.

You never know when a follow-up call is going to bring you a sale. Just keep these two quotes in mind:

> *You miss 100 percent of the shots you don't take.*
> —WAYNE GRETZKY

> *Every no brings you one step closer to a yes.*
> —Every sales guru who has ever lived, but I'm
> going to attribute it to my hero, ZIG ZIGLAR

It's just the truth. Every follow-up call gets you one step closer to your next sale.

So the real questions are these:

- How badly do you need to win?
- How much do you want it?
- How important is success?

I would take Seth Godin's advice on this one. "Quit or be exceptional. Average is for losers."

YOUR COMMITMENT

Can you get by in sales without mastering the discipline of follow-up?

Well, yes . . . if "get by" is your goal.

But true sales rock stars choke on the very concept of "get by." "Get by" is a losing strategy reserved for low achievers and sales moochers. *That's not you!*

You are way better than that, and you deserve more than the scraps that mediocre salespeople are fighting over. Follow up and close the sale!

Time for some honesty. Complete these lines.

"I used to think that follow-up was . . ."

_____

_____

_____

_____

"From now on, I will choose to see follow-up as . . ."

_____

_____

_____

_____

Your follow-up mindset will make all the difference in the world, and you'll be on the quick path to changing your customer's world.

Self-Study Questions:

1. How do you show your customers you care about them? List specific actions, not just polite words.

2. How well are you aligned with the core mindset of relationship-based and service-driven follow-up? Think of one customer and describe both elements.

3. Reflect on a recent major purchase you considered. What other elements of life got in the way between when you talked with the salesperson and when you finally made the purchase . . . or forgot about it?

4. When do you tend to stop making follow-up calls? First, second, or third attempt? What sales do you think you're missing out on?

5. What are the myths you tell yourself about not doing follow-up? How does this mental dialogue hold you back from making sales?

Now Do This:

Consider purchasing a blank journal to keep with you as you read this book. Jot down your thoughts, concerns, fears, questions, and misgivings. This will help you to read with a greater sense of intentionality.

2

Falling in Love with Follow-Up

*People don't buy from you because you
bother them; they buy from you because
you care more than anyone else.*

THE CUSTOMER'S BUYING JOURNEY

CUSTOMER: "I need to think about it. I'll get back to you. I love the bike, but I need some time."

SALESPERSON: "I understand. It's a big decision because it's a really nice bike. Is there anything in particular that I can clarify for you to help in that process?"

CUSTOMER: "Nope. You've done a good job providing me with all the details. I need to run some numbers and see how this fits into my budget; it is definitely more than I want to spend. I want to take one more look at my other options before I make a decision."

SALESPERSON: "You realize that I cannot protect the price and terms that I've already offered, unless you were to decide to buy it today. Is that worth considering?"

CUSTOMER: "I understand, and I appreciate your diligence. But I am 100 percent not moving forward today, with you or with anyone else."

SALESPERSON: "Fair enough. I'm here whenever you need me. I really do think we have the best bike for your situation."

CUSTOMER: "Thanks for the help. I'll be in touch."

What could happen next, from the *salesperson's* perspective:

- Walks away feeling positive about the interaction and the value.
- Feels proud of doing his best, giving a solid presentation, asking for the sale, and persisting when the customer said he wanted to think about it.
- Mentally chalks up a future sale.
- Tells the store owner he might as well count the sale; it is as good as done.
- Tells an interested customer later that day that the bike is "on hold."

What could happen next, from the *customer's* perspective:

- Walks away feeling positive about the interaction and the value.
- Runs the numbers and likes what he sees.
- Is still concerned about how much he will need to spend. Decides to sleep on it.
- Has a bad day at work. His stress level skyrockets, and that triggers a two-day migraine.
- Weeks go by, and he barely remembers the conversation with the bike salesperson.

What happened? What fundamental follow-up mistake was made by the salesperson?

It is a mistake that gets made over and over again by sales practitioners around the globe every single day. Two mistakes, actually:

1. The salesperson put the burden of the next step on the shoulders of the customer.
2. The salesperson never followed up.

How often is that story repeated in different sales scenarios each day?

The reality is that purchase decisions are emotion based, and in the lack of follow-up that emotion wanes. In time a once-strong prospect will have completely forgotten that he or she was ever interested at all.

REVISITING EMOTIONAL ALTITUDE

I touched on this concept in Chapter 1, and I will elaborate further now. One of the most important concepts you must understand about your customer's journey is what goes on in the buying brain. You need to understand Emotional Altitude (EA), which can be defined as the level of positive emotional involvement in a situation or a decision.

A marriage proposal should be a time of high Emotional Altitude. Enjoying a reunion with an old friend makes for elevated EA. So does a really good meal served by an attentive and friendly food server. Buying a really cool jacket or a piece of sports memorabilia or a new car—all should be times of high Emotional Altitude.

It is important to note that the distinction here is not between positive emotion and negative emotion. Rather, the distinction is between positive emotion versus *no* emotion. The absence of emotion makes for an unremarkable setting in which to make a purchase decision.

Why is EA so important? To answer this question, we have to understand how much of the buying decision is based on emotion and how much on logic.

On my podcast, *The Buyer's Mind*, I interview psychologists, behavioral economists, and top-level marketers to try to understand the way people make purchase decisions. (Listen at jeffshore.com/podcast or search for it on iTunes.)

One of the most fascinating guests I've had on the show was the Danish researcher Martin Lindstrom, a renowned expert in the study of consumer psychology. In an extensive research study, Lindstrom observed people's brains through an fMRI while those study participants were making purchase decisions. He could literally see which part of the brain was firing when purchase decisions were being made. He found that (drum roll, please . . .) 85 percent of the decision is based on emotion and 15 percent is based on logic.

Yes, 85 percent! That is a staggering number. It tosses out the kitchen window much of what we have believed about sales, not to mention a good chunk of the content that sales trainers have taught over the years.

Let me show you on a timeline, using the example from the start of this chapter (see figure).

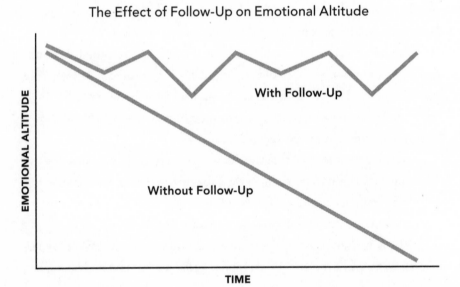

The Effect of Follow-Up on Emotional Altitude

Key point: The farther your customer is removed from the initial emotional experience, the more the Emotional Altitude wanes. And when the EA plummets far enough, you will fall out of your customer's emotional memory altogether.

WHAT YOUR CUSTOMER NEEDS FROM YOU

There is a remedy to this situation: to purposefully and strategically sustain a high degree of EA. How do you do that? You guessed it: follow-up.

Your customer *needs* you to follow up, but not so that you can burden her with statistics and information and data that you think is cool but actually serves to overwhelm her brain. What your customer needs is your assistance in helping her to stay emotionally engaged.

Like everything else in the sales process, this isn't about you. This is not about following up to get the sale. It's not about staying out of trouble. It's not about checking the box in the CRM. Follow-up is about serving your customer by enhancing her Emotional Altitude.

Think like a customer. Why would *you* want a salesperson to follow up?

> You can't stay in your corner of the Forest
> waiting for others to come to you. You
> have to go to them sometimes.
>
> —A. A. MILNE, *Winnie-the-Pooh*

Consider the scenario from the beginning of this chapter. Our customer wants to purchase a bike. Why? What got him excited about that idea in the first place? Perhaps it was to get in shape. Maybe he was bored with his in-home workout equipment or he has a dream about one day biking across France.

Whatever that motivation was, did it change? Did his problem somehow get solved? Or does he still need a bike? He may have gotten distracted along the way. His Emotional Altitude might have dropped. But he is still a prospective bike purchaser, correct? What would he need from a salesperson?

He would need further communication that is:

- Relationship based: It extends the strong rapport that was already established.
- Service driven: The customer needs to know that the salesperson has his best interests at heart.
- Emotionally positive: That emotional fire needs to be rekindled.

With that in mind, is there room for a follow-up call? *Yes!*

ARE YOU "PALMS UP" OR "PALMS DOWN"?

There is one other follow-up perspective for you to consider, and it is critical. I cannot recall where I first heard this, so forgive the lack of citation for this concept, but you have to evaluate whether you are "palms up" or "palms down" in your follow-up efforts.

Picture yourself standing face-to-face with your customer. Now extend both arms toward that prospect. Are you "palms up" or "palms down"?

Palms up means you are coming into that discussion wanting to receive. "Give me something—in this case, a purchase order."

Palms down means you are coming to the discussion wanting to give. "I have this for you; it might help your decision process."

FROM THE FIELD

If you're not (yet) super excited about follow-up, you're not alone. In our field survey only 18 percent of salespeople said they love it. At the other end of the scale, just 3 percent hate it. Most folks, 55 percent, are in the middle. Looks like we have lots of room to get excited, get going, and get giving.

Where is your heart on this? How do you feel about follow-up? Always remember: Follow-up is a giving activity.

THE MINDSET SHIFT

I want to challenge you to change your thinking about sales follow-up. You can begin by adopting the right mindset—namely, that follow-up should be seen as:

- Relationship based
- Service driven
- Emotionally positive

When you carry that mindset and apply the tools, systems, and techniques that follow, you will stand out for all the right reasons. You will prove to your customer that you just care more than everyone else. They will welcome your call, and they will choose to do business with you and only you.

> ### Make a customer, not a sale.
> —KATHERINE BARCHETTI

Remember: *People don't buy from you because you bother them; they buy from you because you care more than anyone else.*

Self-Study Questions:

1. How well are you aligned with the core mindset of relationship-based, service-driven, and emotionally positive follow-up? Think of a time you used all of these in your sales efforts with one customer. Write down how that follow-up unfolded and what outcome you achieved.

2. Think of a recent purchase decision you made. If you're being really honest, what percentage of your decision was based on emotion rather than logic?

3. Recall a recent situation when you intended to buy something, but you were distracted and never completed the purchase. What kind of follow-up did you have from that salesperson? What else could he or she have done?

Now Do This:

Take some time to pull up a couple of old and fairly stale leads. Look at the history of your interactions and the follow-up strategy you followed. Could you honestly describe it as being:

- Relationship based
- Service driven
- Emotionally positive

What lessons can you learn from those interactions?

Now take those lessons and apply them to an active prospect. Do it now while you are thinking about it and the concept is fresh in your brain. Track your results and see if it doesn't make an immediate impact.

3

Fighting Resistance

*As a sales professional you must learn
to fight through the imposing barrier
called Resistance. You must have a solid
mental strategy to defeat this enemy.*

GETTING STARTED

It's time to make some follow-up calls. Let's see, what else is it time
to do?

- Fill out your commission report.
- Catch up on emails.
- Check social media. (Bound to find some leads there, right?)
- Check Google News to see which country invaded which other
  country.
- Watch an inspirational video on YouTube (to get pumped up for
  your follow-up calls, of course).
- Watch a Fail Blog video on YouTube. (Hey, you were already
  there, so why not?)
- Floss your teeth.
- Check social media again.

- Retweet a hilarious Reddit.com post.

- Stare into space wondering what would happen if aliens invaded.

- Pull up your Ring Video Doorbell to see if your Amazon package has arrived.

- Spend 40 minutes on Amazon researching noise-cancelling headphones.

- Hey, you're off in 20 minutes. You don't have time for follow-up calls.

OK, so it's not that bad. In fact, it's *never* that bad for sales professionals who understand the value and benefits of a solid follow-up program. Top performers get into the habit of follow-up. They don't have time to sit around and dream up excuses.

THE NUMBERS DON'T LIE

The statistics on sales follow-up are disturbing to say the least. Here are a few telling tidbits:[1]

- 50 percent of sales happen after the fifth contact.

- The average sales rep only makes two attempts to reach a prospect.

- 44 percent of salespeople give up after one follow-up.

- 92 percent of salespeople give up after no sales on the fourth call.

- 60 percent of customers say no four times before saying yes.

Two opposing forces wage war in the brains of sales professionals everywhere. In one corner stands the fan favorite, the perfect specimen of accomplishment and success: Achievement Drive. In the other corner stands the villain: Resistance.

RESISTANCE

If you've never read the modern masterpiece *The War of Art* by Steven Pressfield, you are missing out. Pressfield introduces us to Resistance, an invisible but incredibly powerful force that stands in the way of productivity and accomplishment.

> *Resistance is not a peripheral opponent. Resistance arises from within. It is self-generated and self-perpetuated. Resistance is the enemy within.*
>
> —STEVEN PRESSFIELD

Resistance comes in many forms and goes by many names. Procrastination, fear, lack of confidence, excuses, distractions . . . all are the handiwork of Resistance.[2]

Resistance can be described in a number of ways, but consider its common underpinning. Resistance is a result of our comfort addictions.

I wrote an entire book on this subject (*Be Bold and Win the Sale*), but here is the short version: We all love to be comfortable, and we are all hardwired to escape discomfort. Until we learn to manage our comfort addictions, we will forever be at risk of defeat at the hands of Resistance.

Here are a few comfort addictions that pertain directly to salespeople:

- Procrastination: You don't tend to procrastinate on what you find comfortable. Your favorite team is playing; you watch. It's *discomfort* that triggers procrastination.

- Telephobia: This fear affects more salespeople than you think. Many salespeople excel at face-to-face encounters but struggle when it comes to making phone calls. So they don't. That's a comfort addiction. (I'll address this issue in Chapter 10.)

- Objections: The customer raises a concern over a value issue or about a negative online review or something to do with product specifications. How you respond to—or choose to avoid—the objection indicates the degree of comfort addiction.

- Fear of closing: For many salespeople it's not the lack of a good closing line; those are a dime a dozen. It's the confidence, the mindset, the conviction that are often lacking.

- Discomfort over follow-up: Which is, basically, why I wrote this book.

Of course, not all salespeople carry all of these comfort addictions, and the degree to which they struggle will vary greatly. But it is safe to say that we all struggle with a comfort addiction of some kind. I would encourage you to pick up a copy of *Be Bold and Win the Sale* for a thorough discussion on comfort addictions. I can promise you this: The bold life is satisfying, rewarding, and just plain fun!

FROM THE FIELD

Our survey correspondents told us what keeps them from following up:

- Not enough time: 40 percent
- Not fun: 25 percent
- Low anticipated success rate: 24 percent
- Fear of rejection: 19 percent
- Telephobia: 11 percent

(Yes, that totals more than 100 percent, which makes sense because lots of folks struggle with more than one type of resistance!)

WHAT'S ON THE LINE?

Ignoring the effects of Resistance has been the downfall of more than a few salespeople over the years. For others, facing down Resistance has proven to be the magic formula for success.

There is *so* much on the line in this discussion:

- Your confidence: You will be exponentially more confident when you know how to deal with Resistance *before* you face it.

- Your manager's confidence: Sales leaders have an incredibly deep affection for bold salespeople.

- Your career: As long as you give in to your comfort addictions you will be stuck where you are ... at best. Succumbing to prolonged comfort addictions rarely ends well.

- Your customer's well-being: Let me be clear. Your customers *need* your humble boldness. They *need* you to do your job. They *need* you to serve them by taking them to a place that is difficult to get to otherwise.

UNDERSTANDING RESISTANCE

Resistance is a common phenomenon because our brains are wired for self-protection. The number-one job of the brain: keep us alive.

The problem arises when we misinterpret discomfort as a threat. We come across a discomfort, and it triggers a threat sensitivity. Our primitive and instinctive brain then sends a message to our cognitive brain in the form of an important and urgent directive: *run!*

In our increasingly affluent and comfortable society we have become highly sensitive to emotional threats, and we respond accordingly. In his excellent book *Your Survival Instinct Is Killing You*, Dr. Marc Schoen puts it this way: "Despite the growing ubiquity of comfort in our lives, we have become increasingly oversensitive to discomfort—so much that even subtle adversity and general uneasiness have become capable of inculcating fear and unsettling our physical and emotional health."

It is helpful to keep in mind that your primitive brain is often sending you faulty messages. If you wish to deal with your comfort addiction, it begins with anticipating those messages and deciding in advance how you will respond.

CONQUERING RESISTANCE

In the past I would floss "from time to time" (meaning the day before a dentist appointment). Now I floss daily.

In the past, I would let emails pile up in my inbox by the thousands. Now I empty my inbox every day.

In the past I would make my sales calls late in the day. Now I make them in the morning.

How were these improvements made? By choosing my response to Resistance *before* it rears its ugly head.

If you want to be successful, it begins with understanding that Resistance is a mental construct inside your own brain. You must take control of your own mental approach. Here is the good news: You can. You get to choose your own mindset.

> *Everything else can be taken from a man but one thing: the last of the human freedoms—to choose one's attitude in any given set of circumstances."*
> —Viktor Frankl, *Man's Search for Meaning*

The question is not *how* to deal with Resistance; it is *when* to do so. And the answer is . . . now. Yes, literally, right now.

You see, if I wait until I am staring Resistance in the face and then decide at that point how to respond, my primitive brain will take over with a firm instruction: Bail out.

But if I decide *right now* how I will respond when Resistance pops up, I can make that decision from my rational and logical brain. I can decide my course of action *before* I find myself in that fearful place.

I floss daily because I make a decision on how to respond *before* it is time to respond. I empty my inbox every day because I make a decision *before* I open my emails to deal with each one of them right then and there. I make my sales calls early because I plan my day *before* I am sitting at my desk.

It works in all areas of life, follow-up being no exception. You can decide right this very minute how you will respond when it is time to absolutely crush your next follow-up session.

FROM THE FIELD

We asked, "What keeps you from following up?" One response: "Sometimes I just forget and if I don't remember their specific situation, I don't want to sound stupid so I don't make contact at all." (Hint: Decide right now to beat this bit of Resistance by using skills you'll learn in the next chapters.)

YOU GOT THIS!

Here's an exercise that might help. Stop and think of a moment in your day or week when Resistance is likely to crop up. Making follow-up calls seems like it should be an appropriate example!

So it's time to make calls, and big, bad Resistance is offering a slate of other options for you.

I want you to give Resistance a face. Not someone you know, please, but an ugly face. A scary, mean, unfriendly face.

Got it?

Now I want you to imagine it is time to make your follow-up calls. Picture that ugly face popping up in front of you.

Now pick up a two-by-four and smack Resistance in the side of the head. Hit it so hard that it falls over, clearing the path for you to move forward.

Keep reading, because in the pages that follow I will lay out both the tools and the mindsets that will make it easy, effective, and downright fun to achieve follow-up mastery. Resistance is no match for you, my stellar follow-up friend.

Final note: I fought with Resistance while writing this entire chapter. I've got potential distractions all around me. But I started this writing session by hitting Resistance in the side of the head with a two-by-four. And five minutes later I did it again. And again shortly after that.

Resistance is an enemy that is only as strong as you allow it to be. You have the choice to be better and stronger than it—and the choice is yours alone.

Here lies Resistance. May it Rest in Peace.

Self-Study Questions:

1. What are the major ways that Resistance manifests itself for you?

2. Think about other parts of your life where you have conquered Resistance. How did you do it?

3. To what other aspects of your life can you apply conquering Resistance? You might as well use this mindset change for even greater benefit!

4. Did you do the two-by-four exercise at the end of the chapter? Did you overcome Resistance and complete your follow-up calls? If so, give yourself a reward . . . and carry on!

Now Do This:

Pick one element of Resistance that limits your follow-up efforts now. Where do you face discomfort when it comes time to follow up? Identify that moment and write it down.

What response can you select *in advance* to hit this part of Resistance with a two-by-four?

PART II
STRATEGY

4

Setting Up the Follow-Up

*Too many salespeople think of follow-up
as an isolated step that takes place down
the road. But a sale is better considered as
one extended narrative, a conversation that
begins with the first point of contact and
continues through the purchase process.*

DO YOU REALLY *NEED* TO FOLLOW UP?

In a book devoted entirely to the practice of follow-up, it might seem rather bizarre for me to suggest that, in a perfect world, this is something you really should not do. In a perfect world, the prospect makes a purchase decision at the conclusion of the presentation and no follow-up is ever needed.

While the practice of follow-up remains a critical discipline and a habit that you must master, I would be remiss if I didn't remind you that your first choice will always be to go for the yes during the initial encounter.

We're all in agreement on that? Good! Let's move on.

You want to go for the sale on that initial presentation, most certainly. But if the prospect says, "Not yet," the follow-up process must kick in—urgently and thoroughly.

THE URGENCY OF FOLLOW-UP

People buy on emotion and support their decision with logic. We are emotion-driven creatures at heart, and we rely on that emotional impulse to spur us on. According to Nobel Prize winner Daniel Kahneman, when we rob people of their emotional impulse, they make poorer-quality decisions.

What does the presence of emotion have to do with follow-up?

Follow-up shortens the buying cycle. That's important because the longer people stay in the purchase process without buying, the further removed they become from that initial emotional impulse. They move into the analytics zone and become mentally paralyzed by the data and the details. In time they are less likely to make the deal.

The concern we are dealing with could be thought of as emotional detachment. The longer people stay in the decision-making loop, the more likely they are to become unmoored from the emotional impulse.

That means there is a directive to you, the sales professional, to shorten the buying cycle. You must do everything in your power to get to the close as quickly as you can.

> *Damn the torpedoes! Full speed ahead!*
>
> —David Farragut

Consider this scenario. You're in a store and you see a great pair of shoes. You absolutely love the shoes, and you can picture yourself rocking those kicks with a favorite pair of jeans. But the shoes are well outside your shoe-price paradigm. You think that $X is a lot of money for a pair of shoes, and these shoes are $100 *more* than $X.

If you are going to purchase those expensive shoes, you are most likely to buy them right then. If you decide to walk away and "think about it," the chances that you will eventually purchase the shoes will plummet.

Why? Because time has a way of separating us from the emotional impulse we need in order to make the decision in the first place.

EXTENDING THE CONVERSATION

It might take days, weeks, or months for a prospect to make a final decision, but you want to envision the entirety of the sales process as one long conversation. Your purpose in that extended conversation is to fuel the emotional momentum.

Too many salespeople see the sales process as a series of disconnected conversations. The various sales discussions you will hold along the way should not be seen as a succession of independent conversations but rather as one long dialogue.

The best way to do that is by planning for an extended chat from the start. Your follow-up will be so much stronger if you are planning for your next conversation during the initial presentation. And during that follow-up conversation you should be planning what happens next . . . and so on. This is a progressive strategy formed in real time as you look for ways to set up future follow-up discussions.

My friend Mike Kunkle puts this quite nicely: "The best advice I can offer for following up with a prospect after the initial appointment is to set the follow-up meeting *during* that first appointment. A mentor shared the acronym HAM-BAM with me over 25 years ago. It stands for Have A Meeting, Book A Meeting. In between the meetings, it helps to send a summary of your notes from the first meeting, detailing what you learned—especially about any challenges they're experiencing and what they hope to accomplish and why—and including the agenda, goals, and expected outcomes for the next meeting."

This helps you:

- Get to know the customer better by asking deeper questions
- Learn details that other salespeople will miss
- Identify problems that will need to be solved
- Gain agreements on next steps

DURING THE PRESENTATION

Make no mistake. When it comes to sales, the little things are the big things. Those little gems of information that you gather along the way will help you piece together a comprehensive and personalized follow-up strategy.

This is why I encourage you to take a lot of notes. And not just to record price preferences or feature needs. Jot down information about hobbies, family, schooling, and other interests. The fact is that you never know what is going to help you reconnect down the road.

The last time I was in for a checkup, my dentist asked me about an important project that I had been working on six months prior. Now look, I am well aware that he wrote it down and checked his notes before I came in for the visit; there is no way he could remember all the details six months later. Do you think that bothered me? Not at all! He cared enough to jot it down.

Taking notes during the presentation can be particularly helpful when identifying pain points. Problem-solving is a great way to add value in your follow-up.

Example #1

Your client has a boss who will greatly influence the decision, and you discover that the boss hates salespeople. Knowing this pain point can help you craft a strategy to win that boss over, perhaps by sending valuable intel that will make the organization more profitable. For example, show how the synergy of your product or service, combined with the client's product, create a highly competitive value proposition.

Example #2

You learn that your buyer raises show dogs and travels with the dogs extensively. Knowing that information, how could you provide creative information that would benefit your prospect in some way? Perhaps you could share a website or blog that identifies dog-friendly hotels, restaurants, parks, and other spots around the country.

Example #3

A new home salesperson in Atlanta learned that a soon-to-be-single mom had two kids learning karate. This poor lady was going through a divorce and a home-buying decision at the same time. As a part of the follow-up, the sales professional did the research to find the highest-rated karate studios in her area. One less thing for the mom to have to handle.

Example #4

An industrial supply sales professional in Boston learned that a brand-new restaurant was opening near the shop of a prospective client. He went to the restaurant and negotiated a great deal on gift certificates for his would-be client to get some free lunches for his team.

One important key: Look for opportunities to engage the customer's emotion. I'm not talking about being sappy or syrupy. This is about connecting people with their emotional impulse, that magical place where the decisions are actually made. It's OK to give the prospect permission to enjoy the process.

> **FROM THE FIELD**
>
> We asked our survey group how skilled they were at follow-up, and 12 percent said they were superheroes. (That's great!) *Not one* of these superhero salespeople said doing follow-up was *not fun.* Yup, that's a double negative, which might just mean these folks *are* having fun following up with their customers!

AT THE WRAP-UP

As I mentioned at the beginning of the chapter, you should be looking for opportunities to ask for the sale, right from that first conversation. Here is an approach taken from my book *Closing 2.0* that might help you.

It's called the Next Step Close. It is simple, conversational, and logical. It sounds like this:

"So glad to know that you like what you are seeing. The very next step in the process is to sit down and write a purchase agreement. Is that where we are? Is that what you want to do?"

It is a simple question demanding a simple yes-or-no response. The key is to ask in a very easygoing and conversational manner. If it comes off heavy-handed, it will fail.

If the customer says yes, celebrate your new deal.

If the customer says no (or, more accurately, "not yet"), you need to immediately gain mutual commitment for the next step or steps in the process.

Flesh out the reason for the objection and determine whether there is any way to keep the conversation active. If not, lay out the next steps right there. Think to yourself, "How can I best serve this person in my follow-up? What would be most helpful?"

The key is that you, the sales professional, must own the next action. Too often salespeople allow the customer to dictate what will happen next.

The prospect says, "I need to talk to _____," or "I need to investigate _____."

The weaker salesperson will allow the prospect to determine what happens next. The stronger salesperson will jump in and help solve the problem.

Make the next steps cooperative. I am a big fan of using this phrase to set up the follow-up: "Let's do this . . ."

"Let's do this" implies that you both play a role and you both have action items. This keeps the sales process active and allows for a natural introduction of the next interaction.

The critical technique is to make sure that "Let's do this" extends to include a very specific game plan for the next steps. In practice, it might sound like this:

"OK, so you want to talk to your financial people; I get that. And I want to do some research on how to customize that one feature that would help you. Let's do this: Why don't we regroup on Wednesday afternoon? I'll have all the information you need by then. Does ten o'clock work for you?"

THE LAST IMPRESSION

Once you have agreed upon the next steps, you want to make sure that the conversation ends on a strong and positive note. People remember how experiences end. That finale, when done properly, can have a strong impact on memory, often overshadowing everything else that happened earlier.*

My wife and I dined recently at The French Laundry in Yountville, California. (Yes, we *dined*. One does not simply *eat* at those prices.) When we were leaving, the hostess met us at the door, thanked us by name, and

---

* The peak–end rule is a psychological heuristic in which people judge an experience largely based on how they felt at its peak (i.e., its most intense point) and at its end, rather than based on the total sum or average of every moment of the experience.

handed us a folder that detailed the dinner we had, where the ingredients came from, and who cooked our meal. A wonderful way to add a memorable touch.

Get creative with this. It might be worth your time to think about how you say goodbye and what you can do to become more memorable. Remember that the next step for the prospect might be to investigate other options. How you become memorable at the end of the conversation can have a huge effect on how you stand out at the end of the day.

THE VERY NEXT MOMENT

How soon is too soon when it comes to follow-up? It depends on what you are doing, but when done properly, it is *never* too soon to be memorable.

My hot tip? I call it "taillight follow-up."

Suppose you are in a retail environment and you can literally see your customer pull away from your parking lot. You see the taillights. (The principle still works if you see customers walking away or if you've just left their office.)

Pull out your cell phone and fire off a text message that sounds something like this:

"I enjoyed that conversation. I'll call you by 10 a.m. tomorrow." What did you just accomplish?

- You let customers know they matter.
- You stood out from everyone else.
- You confirmed the appointment for the next step.
- You demonstrated you're a person who takes action.
- You showed respect with immediate follow-up.
- You put your phone number onto their cell phone.

Score times six!

USE THE CRM

Then what? Sit down and get their data into your customer relationship management system, whether it's a notebook you keep on your desk or a complex electronic CRM system. The longer you wait, the more that information goes bad on you. Don't rely on your memory to keep track of important details!

But it's not just remembering the details; it's also remembering how you feel. Enter the information into the CRM *while YOUR emotional energy is high*. You will write better notes and develop a better plan if you are still high on a truly great encounter!

Write the juicy stuff. Include the tiny details. Jot down what will make you *want* to follow up.

Self-Study Questions:

1. How well do you know your customers? Pick two customers and write down as many things as you can think of about them. Not the product you want to try to sell them, but the people themselves. How does this help you plan your next follow-up?

2. How would you feel if you received a "taillight text" after leaving a sales meeting where you were the prospective buyer? Use these feelings to help you tailor your own taillight follow-up messages to be sincere, meaningful, positive, and value-adding—in 140 characters or less.

3. Think of your typical non-close sales discussion. How can you modify your approach to end on a high note?

4. Think of one of your current selling relationships, someone you're doing active follow-up with. Identify a pain point for this customer and a creative way that you can help solve the customer's problem.

5. Some people are uncomfortable taking notes during a discussion, but you *need* that information. How are you going to communicate tactfully to the customer that you're going to take notes? Good. Practice this so it doesn't seem awkward.

Now Do This:

This week, concentrate on ending every sales conversation by setting up the next conversation. Track your results and mark your progress as you go. Notice how setting up the follow-up makes a huge impact on both you and your customer.

5

How *Not* to Get Eliminated

*Elimination is a thinning-out strategy.
Avoiding elimination is critical to
being able to stay in the game.*

TOO MANY CHOICES

Larry is in the market for a new television for his bonus room. He has a 40-inch flat screen in the room at present, but it's not big enough. Larry loves football and wants a far bigger and top-of-the-line quality screen for him and his soon-to-be-envious friends to enjoy. This purchase will be pricey and not altogether essential; it is an extravagant luxury.

Larry begins his buying journey reading online reviews, checking Amazon and CNET, and trying to get a feel for how to balance the debate between size, picture quality, and price. On a visit to Costco, he spends 30 minutes moving from television to television. At Best Buy he stops to look at no less than 10 sets.

The problem: There are simply too many choices. Larry's head will explode if he attempts to do a comparison of every television at every price.

The solution: Eliminate options.

HOW THE BRAIN PROCESSES INFORMATION

We humans have advanced brains. We can process a great deal of information. But it's so much easier and a lot less of a headache if we narrow our options. Barry Schwartz, author of *The Paradox of Choice: Why More Is Less*, says, "A greater variety of choices actually makes us feel worse. By restricting our options, we will be able to choose less and feel better."[1]

That makes sense for Larry who is trying to decide which TV to buy. It makes sense for a young couple in the market for a new home. It even makes sense for the purchasing agent in a multinational manufacturing operation.

> *A confused mind says no.*
>
> —ANONYMOUS

Elimination of choices is a common and legitimate purchase decision strategy. You probably knew that instinctively, but let's get into the psychology behind all this.

The brain processes information at an impressively high rate. The room where you are sitting at this moment has countless data points coming at you at the same time.

Most of that data is processed in the nonconscious part of the brain. As you read this, you are probably not paying attention to the ambient sounds in the room (air conditioning, computer fan, refrigerator, etc.). Oh, wait— now you are. The sounds were there the entire time; I just elevated them from nonconscious to conscious status.

This handy little brain strategy is a part of what the experts call dual-process theory. The brain processes the overwhelming amount of available information via the nonconscious. Only a small portion of our decisions are made in the conscious brain.

What does this tell us for follow-up? Keep your presence visible, out there in front of the nonconscious part of the brain, but keep things simple.

THE LAW OF LEAST EFFORT

Why does dual processing happen? Because the brain is always looking for shortcuts. The brain is an incredible energy-saving machine. It is constantly and creatively identifying ways to simplify.

This is all an attempt on the part of the brain to alleviate cognitive strain, which happens when we have to do a lot of conscious processing of information. The fact is that decision-making is far easier in moments of cognitive ease, when we rely on what *feels* right, sometimes even without thinking much about making a decision.

In fact, the brain follows a simple but powerful psychological hack:

$$Easy = Right$$

The easier something seems to me, the more right it feels to me.

This is why so many companies are structuring their processes to make it easy for a customer to do business with them. Chewy.com has a set-it-and-forget-it strategy for how to buy pet food. Many car dealers have initiated fixed pricing with no haggling. Indochino even makes it easy to purchase a custom-made suit.

To the customer, easy = right.

CONNECTING THE DOTS

So, where does the elimination strategy fit in all this? Elimination is the easy way to simplify offerings, and that shortcut provides us with significant cognitive ease (and easy = right, right?).

Let's go back to Larry for a moment, as he continues his television shopping adventure. He has far too many choices, and that makes for cognitive strain. His brain will search for a decision-making shortcut in order to alleviate some of that overload. Larry's brain will send him into elimination mode. He will begin to eliminate some of his options in order to set the table for an easier decision. But here's where it gets really interesting. Larry will begin eliminating options . . . and he won't even know it.

That's right—most of the elimination process takes place subconsciously. If it doesn't look right or if it doesn't feel right or if it doesn't trigger a positive emotion, the buyer will make quick subconscious decisions to eliminate the option. There is a reason all the televisions in the store are showing dramatic scenes of the Italian coastline or an African safari or an action-packed football game. The goal is to trigger a positive and dramatic response.

We could put this elimination process in Marie Kondo terms: Does something bring you joy? If not, it's out of consideration.[2] That joy moves us forward; the absence of joy causes us to scuttle the option.

A quick note to marketers: This elimination strategy takes place in the simplest of ways. Sloppy wording on a website. Poor product displays. Abrasive colors. Any or all of these unintended "features" can lead to quick and nonconscious elimination. The tiny details matter!

> *DWYSYWD stands for Do What You Say You Will Do . . . Don't say "I'll call back tomorrow" unless you will call back tomorrow. Deliver proposals on time. Find the answers you said you'd get. Preserve your credibility by doing what you say you will do.*
>
> —Deb Calvert

TWO TYPES OF ELIMINATION

When it comes to do sales follow-up, there are two very different types of elimination:

1. Active elimination: "I hate that product and I'm not buying it." This occurs when prospects make a conscious and reasoned decision to reject a specific offering. The price is too high. The specs are wrong. They just plain didn't like it all that much.

2. Passive elimination: "I forgot all about those guys!" This occurs when an offering simply falls from a prospect's mind. Your average customer has a million things to think about on any given day. The more time that elapses without a refreshing of the offering, the more likely it is that the customer will just plain forget about that option.

Active elimination is going to happen. We can't be all things to all people. But passive elimination is an unforgivable sales sin. We must never through neglect and inattention fall out of the consciousness of our prospects.

Follow-up is your safety net against passive elimination. And, most important, it is completely within your own control!

Remember the story earlier in the book about the ghostwriter who offered to help me and then disappeared? What happened that caused me to reject that service offering? Passive elimination. There was no follow-up, so I simply forgot about the service as a viable option. By the time I did get some follow-up, I was already committed to—and excited about—a different path. (Our next chapter explains why *speed* of follow-up is so important.)

Sales follow-up is your protection against passive elimination. The prospect might eliminate you for all kinds of legitimate reasons. After all, we cannot be all things to all people. But passive elimination must never be the reason that a customer says no.

If customers forget about you, you're sunk. It's really that simple. And if you fail to recontact as you should, they will surely forget.

On the other hand, follow-up—when done properly—is happily memorable. Customers appreciate the efforts of a helpful sales professional because it keeps them connected to the product they love and are seriously considering. In fact, follow-up helps the customer to eliminate *other* options. Take that, competitors!

YOUR STRATEGY FOR AVOIDING ELIMINATION

Fortunately, the path to avoiding elimination is not that difficult. It really comes down to one word: consistency. If you are systematic in your approach and if you devote just a short time every single day to the effort, you can avoid the trap that so many salespeople fall into.

Suppose you are selling janitorial services to a company that owns several office buildings. You make your initial pitch and you send a quick email by way of a thank you. Then suppose you do absolutely nothing for the next 30 days, at which time you send a second email.

In that 30-day period your potential client has likely talked to several competitors, vetted the choices, and made a decision. And even if no decision has yet been made, it doesn't matter; so much time has lapsed that the prospective client has forgotten about you. You lose the deal because you are, in essence, a total stranger. The prospect doesn't even remember your name!

To avoid elimination do the following religiously:

- Review your strongest leads every day.
- Review all your leads at least once a week.

Get into the daily habit of asking yourself, "How can I move this sale along today? What can I do to eliminate the barriers to a purchase decision?"

That constant focus will go a long way toward staying active, creative, and motivated to get that sale across the finish line. Consistent follow-up keeps the customer emotionally engaged.

Jeffrey Gitomer, author of *The Sales Bible*, says, "I think the faster you follow up, the more wow there is in the sales process."

Starting with that early follow-up and maintaining a consistent pattern of value-added communication keeps you in the game, with a little "wow" in every interaction. It's hard to be forgotten when you're right there in front of the customer at every turn.

FROM THE FIELD

Krystal Land is a perfect example of how important follow-up is. She did *not* let herself be eliminated. "I kept following up with someone for one year and they finally bought from me. Patience is a virtue."

My wish for you is that you become absolutely paranoid about passive elimination. I don't want you to sleep well if customers are slipping away when you could have done something about it.

Resistance is real. Resistance will tell you to let those prospects go.

Be better than Resistance. Be the champion your customer needs you to be!

Self-Study Questions:

1. Think about the last five times you lost a potential sale. Was each due to active elimination or passive elimination?

2. For one of your past missed sales that was due to passive elimination, after reading this chapter, what would you do differently now?

3. Imagine you're the customer. Think of the last time you shopped around for a big-ticket item. What did the salespeople do or not do

that got their product or service eliminated? What did the winning salesperson do?

4. Which is easier? Doing the follow-up work to keep a customer engaged or trying everything under the sun to get a customer reengaged once you've been passively eliminated?

5. Apply the idea of eliminating passive elimination in your personal life. Pick an area where you're being ignored or forgotten and take bold action.

Now Do This:

I want to throw out a challenge to you right now. Seriously, read this section, and then put the book down and do the activity while the idea is fresh in your brain.

Think about your five prospects that are most in danger of passive elimination, who might just forget about you if you do not follow up soon. What can you do to reengage those prospects *right now*? How can you reignite the relationship? What would stir their emotions? How can you serve them best?

Be bold. Be daring. If you picked prospects who were in danger of elimination, you were about to lose them anyway. Why not take some chances? What's the worst thing that can happen?

6

Speed: Your Secret Superpower

Your customers have a miniscule attention span, and they can forget you in no time at all if you wait too long to initiate a follow-up sequence. Speed is your secret weapon when it comes to extending the relationship and keeping customers engaged.

THE POWER OF SPEED

Jennifer goes on a date with a young man named Pete—a blind date, actually. Pete is the brother of Jennifer's coworker.

The duo head out for Italian food, followed by a visit to a local coffee house. Everything goes really well. Pete asks for Jennifer's phone number and she obliges, borrowing a pen from a barista and writing the number on the insulation sleeve of her coffee cup.

The next day Jennifer is reflecting on the pleasant evening . . . while waiting for the phone to ring.

No call.

No call on the next day either. Or the day after that.

What is Jennifer thinking at this point?

Three weeks later Jennifer goes out with Mario, a guy she barely knows from her church. They have a great conversation about a variety of topics, including a discussion of their mutual appreciation for quality dark chocolate. Mario walks her home, asks for her number, and says good night.

An hour later Jennifer receives a text from Mario that reads, "Check your front porch." On the porch sits a stack of five different dark chocolate bars with a note that reads, "I like you. You're sweet. Let's get together soon."

What is Jennifer thinking at this point?

DATING AND SALES

Dating and sales. They have a lot in common, when you think about it. But the greatest commonality by far is the presence of emotion in both situations. People date on emotion. And people buy on emotion.

FROM THE FIELD

Molly Jacobs, a client relationship manager with Ernest Packaging, says: "The sales process . . . is very similar to dating. After my initial process call, I'll follow up, like texting after the first date. Had a great time. Can't wait to see you again."

In both cases an important principle is at play, which I address in Chapter 2: Emotional Altitude.

We purchase in times of high Emotional Altitude. Buying is an emotional decision, 85 percent emotional. In the absence of that emotion, it is very difficult to make a decision.

As it relates to sales follow-up, this begs an important question: What is the biggest factor in sustaining Emotional Altitude after the initial sales presentation?

Speed.

SPEED

We love speed. We are pleasantly surprised when we encounter speedy service. We appreciate prompt attention at the restaurant or the mechanic's workshop or the doctor's office. We live in an instant gratification culture.

Why is this so important to sales professionals? Because *customers equate speed with great service.* They believe that service providers care more when they are quick to resolve a problem or offer an insight.

> ### FROM THE FIELD
>
> Don't take this advice just from me. One of our survey respondents gave this as her number-one best follow-up tip: "Reaching out immediately and making my clients say, '*Wow*, that was fast!'" Another said, "I make my first contact within one hour. When I am able to do this, my response rates soar."

We read a lot of things into speed:

- "He cares."
- "I matter."
- "I can trust her."
- "He is attentive."
- "She likes me."

THE SPEED TREND

Entire organizations are built around the principle of speed. Here are three:

Amazon (Especially Amazon Prime)

I don't know how much I pay for my Amazon Prime account, and frankly, I don't much care. All I know is that I can order something with one click and get it the next day (and in some cases, the same day). In our instant gratification society, that's important.

Amazon had a real challenge when it came to cutting into the business of brick-and-mortar stores. It did it by providing a superior service, and speed is the key to that service.

UberEATS

We all know how Uber changed the private transportation industry. Those same drivers have made meal delivery more convenient and surprisingly fast.

Mystery shopping firm SeeLevel HX evaluated the promptness of a number of meal delivery services and found that UberEATS deliveries took on average 35 minutes from the placing of the order to the delivery of the meal.[1] Thirty-five minutes. I've waited much longer than that sitting in a restaurant waiting for a server to carry my meal 100 feet.

The convenience of the service is great. The fact that it can be accomplished in such a short time is what wins customers.

ERs Throughout the United States

The average wait time in a US hospital emergency room has plummeted over the years. In fact, last year 59 major hospitals in the country boasted of wait times of *less than four minutes*. This is a prime example of speed being translated as care.

If there is ever a time when you want things done quickly, it's when you're ailing. When we evaluate the quality of service in an emergency room, speed of care is a factor at the top of the list.

THE CURE

Speed is the cure for passive elimination. Recall from our last chapter that as time elapses after a sales conversation you become more and more forgettable, leading to the point where your prospects passively eliminate you as a viable option.

On the other hand, the benefits of speed are varied and powerful:

- You show you care.

- You stand out.

- You interrupt your competitor's presentation.

- You surprise people.

- You are more memorable.

- You feel good.

- You get a competitive advantage.

- You extend the relationship.

- You get more sales!

Research by sales acceleration firm Velocify shows that speed-to-call is the most important factor in determining whether you contact or convert an interested prospect.[2]

Going further, research featured in the *Harvard Business Review* even suggests that companies that follow up within an hour with customers are as much as *seven times* more likely to qualify their leads. You don't want to let your best sales leads lose interest or be contacted by a more persistent competitor.[3]

Let's get one thing straight about sales follow-up: 24 hours is a really long time in the life of a busy prospect; 48 hours is an eternity. In 72 hours you never existed.

> *The only thing faster than the speed of thought is the speed of forgetfulness.*
>
> —VERA NAZARIAN

As a sales counselor, you must understand that your prospects are faced with myriad messages all aimed at capturing their attention. So if prospects do not hear from you for 48 hours after a sales conversation, what happens? How many new messages are they bombarded with in those 48 hours? How far removed are they from your sales presentation? How much else has happened to *you* in those 48 hours?

THE REMEDY: FOUR HOURS

We surveyed hundreds of sales professionals to get data on what people are doing in the real world. We asked, "How quickly do you follow up after the first visit?" The response was overwhelming, with 90 percent saying they follow up the same day or the next day (survey results listed below).

- Within one hour: 17 percent
- Same day: 45 percent
- The next day: 27 percent
- Within a week: 9 percent
- Within a month: 2 percent

That's 90 percent of folks making the time in their schedule to follow up within 24 hours. That's a great start.

Do you know what's even greater? Four hours. If a customer leaves your sales office by noon, the first follow-up call should take place later that same day. If a customer leaves the office at 4 p.m., the first follow-up call should be made early the next day.

This book will show you the *how* of follow-up, but you really need to start with the *when*.

The strategy to adopt today:

1. Make an appointment for your first follow-up in less than four hours. (We'll talk about *how* later on. For now, just get into the habit of setting a four-hour timer.)

2. Ask yourself, "What value can I add in the next four hours?"

> *The future of sales is realtime. Following up with prospects hours, days, or weeks later is like ignoring a person when they walked into your store and sending them postcards in hopes that they come back. Not very effective.*[4]
>
> —David Cancel

TOO FAST?

One last thing. How fast is too fast? Might you be in danger of damaging the relationship?

That all depends on how much value you bring in your follow-up. If your four-hour call is nothing more than, "Well, have you made a decision yet?" you're not bringing much value to the conversation.

But if you are providing something meaningful, helpful, or caring, then you will have earned the right to a speedy reconnection.

Speed in follow-up is half the strategy. In the next chapter we will add a second secret weapon.

> **FROM THE FIELD**
>
> "Always leave your first appointment with something you can fol-low up with, even if you know the answer! For example, 'I don't know that, but I'll find out and get back to you,' gives you some-thing to break the ice with."

Self-Study Questions:

1. How soon do you typically follow up with a customer?

2. How often do you wait "a while" and then think it's too late to bother following up?

3. Count, or at least estimate, the number of emails, text messages, phone calls, conversations, and crises you had to deal with in the last 24 hours. If you were a customer, would your discussion with a salesperson stay at the top of your mind through all that?

4. How does speed of follow-up give you a competitive advantage?

5. Think of five customers. For each one, identify something meaningful, helpful, or caring you could—and will—share with them as follow-up.

6. What is the worst that could happen if you contact a customer "too soon" with follow-up? Remember this is value-added follow-up, not just, "Hey, how are you doing?"

Now Do This:

This week, focus on four-hour follow-up. Commit to making your first contact in that time window. Note how much easier it is when the relationship is still fresh in the customer's mind. Don't wait—make your first four-hour follow-up call (or text or video) . . . *today!*

7

Making It Personal

Follow-up efforts fail when the customer perceives that the approach is canned, rote, and lacking personal connection. If you want to score big and become powerfully memorable, you need to personalize your communication for each individual prospect.

MAKE YOUR CUSTOMER FEEL IMPORTANT

Mary Kay Ash, the founder of Mary Kay Cosmetics, had an approach that gets at the value of personalization, whether you're selling makeup, new homes, computers, or your own services.

> *Pretend that every single person you meet has a sign around his or her neck that says, "Make me feel important." Not only will you succeed in sales, you will succeed in life.*

Notice that this advice doesn't mention product. Great sales conversations go far beyond a discussion about the product or service. Effective sales calls facilitate a human connection. People are more likely to buy from people they like, and they are more likely to purchase from someone with whom they share a connection.

Suppose you're talking to a prospect and the conversation turns to hobbies. You discover that your prospect took up snowboarding a couple years back and really enjoys it. Let's also suppose that you share that passion. (If you're reading this in Florida and you've never left the state, just use your imagination!)

It's now two hours after the sales call. How can you leverage that small piece of information in your follow-up effort? Perhaps sharing your go-to ski resort review app, information on a multi-resort pass, or a link to a favorite YouTube boarding video. What else can you suggest?

START WITH WHAT YOU HAVE IN COMMON

In the locker room before one of my hockey games there was a lively conversation about motorcycles—specifically, Harley-Davidsons. A newer player on the team joined in with enthusiasm and announced that he rode a Harley-Davidson Fat Boy with a Milwaukee-Eight 114. The other players were most impressed.

Now, I don't know squat about motorcycles of any kind, but it was nonetheless amusing to see the fervor of the conversation. The other players were totally engrossed. Their respect for their teammate soared. Why? Because we gravitate to people who share common interests.

If sales professionals can weave such common interests into the follow-up process they will make a deeply personal connection that will separate them from the competition.

What if you don't have a clear shared interest or hobby? Can you still make a personal connection? Yes, if you are paying attention to the small details during the initial encounter.

I remember years ago when my wife and I were shopping for a home in a city with which I was unfamiliar. I was entertaining a job offer and spent the day visiting an open listing. We had our young daughter with us, and somehow we got into a conversation about my daughter's long hair. I thought we should cut it; my wife disagreed.

When we got back a few days later we found a handwritten note that had been mailed to our home. It was a very kind message from the salesperson we met, but what stood out was a simple line on the bottom of the card. "P.S. Don't cut Emily's hair."

She didn't stop there. She knew that we were unfamiliar with her town, so she sent along a packet of information—these were pre-Internet days—that proved extremely useful in getting to know the lay of the land.

We ended up staying put, but it was her sale to be gained if we had decided to move. I would have literally *wanted* to love her product just because I appreciated her efforts. And how impactful was that follow-up effort? Well, the incident took place in 1991, and I'm still talking about it. You figure it out!

THE SISTER TO SPEED

As I mentioned in the last chapter, speed is half the battle. The other half is personalization.

If you want to stand out in your follow-up effort you must determine how to prove to the customer that you simply out-care any other salesperson at any other company. Personalization is your strategy to accomplishing that goal.

> *If you are not taking care of your customer, your competitor will.*
>
> —BOB HOOEY

The objective here is not simply to make the contact; it is to maximize the quality of the contact. High personalization equates to high perceived quality. The more you personalize your approach, the greater success you will enjoy in your follow-up efforts.

Too many salespeople, in an effort to simply get through the list of follow-up tasks on the CRM, focus on quantity of calls, on "pounding through" the stack rather than on maximizing every conversation. The sales professional who focuses on personalized connection points will find the greatest success in converting sales.

> *Most people think "selling" is the same as "talking." But the most effective salespeople know that listening is the most important part of their job.*
>
> —ROY BARTELL

THE MENTAL APPROACH

Start with the right question: What does your customer need to see for follow-up?

This is a huge mindset shift. This idea implies from the start that effective follow-up is not about the salesperson at all. The goal is to improve the life of the customer.

You can look at follow-up according to what you will *get*, or you can approach it according to what you will *give*. The difference between those two mindsets is the difference between being a nuisance and being a trusted adviser.

> *You have to drop your sales mentality and start working with your prospects as if they've already hired you.*
>
> —JILL KONRATH

So much of follow-up strategy is based on what the company or the salesperson wants. You must take a customer-centric view of sales follow-up. You must "serve" above all else. And the best possible service is *personalized* service.

Ask yourself whether a mindset shift is in order. Have you been approaching follow-up as a task that makes your manager happy? As a means to getting paid? Or a task that you really don't want to do?

Or do you see follow-up as a powerful value-add for your customer?

KNOWING YOUR CUSTOMER

If you want to take that customer-first approach, it begins with knowing your customer well. If you don't know your customer, I can't help you.

Is your discovery deep enough to understand the fine points? How much do you know about your customer's life? Her family? Her interests? Her pets?

I was having a suit made recently, and the conversation turned to favorite podcasts. I informed the salesperson that I had my own podcast. (*The Buyer's Mind*. You should check it out!) He expressed interest in listening to it.

When we met later for the second fitting, he shared with me what he had learned in listening to several episodes. Not only did he bring up specific points of interest, he also asked me about my podcasting history, my enjoyment, and my equipment. He took a genuine interest in something that was important to me. That's great follow-up.

Don't miss this. Our world is so full of impersonal marketing messages. So much sales outreach is based on generic information and lacking personal attention. That means you can stand out in a hurry with minimal effort. Just find and leverage the connection point.

> ### FROM THE FIELD
>
> "The key to successful follow-up is making the connection before your buyer leaves. Find that commonality between you that makes you relatable. Exchanging knowledge or interest in something your buyer is interested in will help you let their guard down. You become a friend not a salesperson, and how easy is it to call a friend? That's my secret sauce!"

KEEPING TRACK

Of course, it's not just what you learn. It's also what you remember. Note-taking offers an important advantage to the top-performing salesperson. Some salespeople find it awkward to take notes while talking to a customer. I see it as a sign of respect.

If you have a hang-up about that you can always say to prospects, "I want to make sure I don't miss anything; do you mind if I jot down some notes?" (They'll say yes, trust me.)

The problem is that when you look at the notes that most salespeople take, you'll find mostly data related to moving the sale down the path: financing needs, product specification requests, time frame, etc. I'm not sure that's going to help you all that much when it comes to personalizing the follow-up.

What kind of information makes for personalized follow-up?

- Understanding interests
- Learning about hobbies
- Discovering personal tastes
- Being observant about small details

- Finding out about family
- Knowing their background and experience

The most important pieces of information for your CRM are the small details that lead to a personal connection with a big payoff in the follow-up process.

FROM THE FIELD

"I write notes about the customer on their contact card regarding their needs and some things that help me identify and remember them. That way the next time I contact them I can reference specific needs or moments to help connect with them personally. For example, 'We have the garage for your motor home and Corvette collection' or 'Your daughter Mindy liked the playroom.'"

These are the types of details that will come up in a conversation if you're truly listening to customers and engaging with them on a personal basis. It's up to you to retain that information and use it effectively to continue the relationship in follow-up.

THINK "CUSTOMIZED"

I want to encourage you to get out of the box and have some fun with this. Think about how to customize every follow-up interaction with a personalized connection point. A little creative effort will go a very long way.

I was working with a research source recently, and I wanted to extend that relationship. So I called her office and talked to her assistant. I asked the assistant about a favorite restaurant, and that very day I sent out a gift card.

The source called the next day and said, "How did you know that was my favorite restaurant? That is so kind of you."

Of course, learning that intel was not difficult in the least. I just had to get creative. (By the way, that consultant has helped me over and over again. Not because of the gift card, but because I cared enough to follow up in a personalized way.)

Clearly, she felt good that I went out of the way to show that I cared. But you know what? It made me feel good, too.

A COUPLE OF CAVEATS

You don't want to appear "stalkerish" by probing deep in your customers' social media. Yes, they've put a lot of information out on the Web for the world to see, but they don't necessarily want *everyone* to repeat it back to them.

Use common sense. Before you refer to any details you've discovered about a customer, think about whether you would want someone to know and use that information about you.

> ### FROM THE FIELD
>
> Here's a learning experience with a heartfelt attempt at personalization with customers: "I assumed a couple that came in were boyfriend and girlfriend. I sent a cute email about buying his sweetheart her dream home for Valentine's Day. Turns out they were father and daughter. Won't do that again!"

Rather than personalizing based on assumptions, use the right approach for questioning, listening, and relating to gather hard details. Take notes and pull that information into follow-up when appropriate.

HAVE FUN!

If you think follow-up is drudgery, personalizing makes it fun. You don't need to sound like a robot; that is far from what your customer is looking for.

Work with your peers on this. Brainstorm ideas and share best practices.

You can *decide* to love follow-up. And it is easiest to do that when you make it personal.

Self-Study Questions:

1. Imagine you're trying to sell something to your best friend, something he or she wants or needs. How would your follow-up message use personalization to help your friend? How could you use that same approach for other buyers who aren't (yet) friends?

2. Besides asking customers outright about personal information, what are other ways to gather useful background . . . without being creepy?

3. How would you strike a balance between incorporating personalization and being productive?

4. What are the dangers of "mass-produced" customization, that is, appearing to personalize without really individualizing your approach?

5. Can you ever overdo it with personalization? How would you know if you're doing too much personalization?

6. What would be a good personalized lead-in for customized follow-up?

7. Personalization doesn't have to be fully one-off. What are some elements of personalization you can use over and over again?

Now Do This:

Pick a customer today and do something to go out of the way to show that you care. That doesn't mean spending money. It's doing something meaningful related to knowing that customer as a person. Okay . . . go!

PART III
EXECUTION

8

Planning for Follow-Up Success

Proper planning—both mental and strategic—produces peak performance. A few minutes spent planning will pay off big-time in developing your strategy and improving your results.

IT ALL STARTS WITH A PLAN

The groundwork is laid, the strategy is in place, and it's time to make your calls. We move now to the meat of the book—the execution. Follow along closely. Go ahead and write notes in the margins. And get ready to rock your follow-up!

THE WRONG WAY TO APPROACH FOLLOW-UP

Picture this quasi-fictional scene with me if you will.

Oh, man. It's 4:30 and I haven't made even one follow-up call today. I was just so busy, what with existing client service, administrative tasks, emails, and constantly responding to dumb questions from my manager, not to mention that accidental 20-minute nap, cleaning my pencil drawer, checking Instagram 67 times, and watching 18 different You-Tube videos showing dogs being reunited with their owners. I mean, how could I possibly have done my follow-up any sooner?'

OK, let me see what pops up on the CRM. OK, it looks like I have, um, 782 follow-up tasks that are overdue. First one? 'Call back the Johanssons to gauge their interest.' Let's see, that task was due . . . 10 days ago. Johansson, Johansson . . . now, who were they exactly? Oh, well. Guess I'll give it a shot (dials).

"Hi, Mr. Johansson, it's Biff Barkley over at Acme Goods and Services. Just calling to see if I can get paid soon . . . I mean, just calling to see if you're ready to buy."

This is obviously a very tongue-in-cheek example . . . at least for top sales professionals! Sadly, for folks who aren't right for sales and who won't stay long in the profession, this may cut a little close to the bone. Whether or not you see some of your own tendencies in that little story, we can all agree there is a better way.

PROPER PLANNING PRODUCES PEAK PERFORMANCE

You wouldn't just show up at your dentist's office without an appointment. You wouldn't start cooking without checking to see that you have the proper ingredients. You wouldn't go on a trip without packing first.

In both life and in sales, proper preparation is everything. You need a plan, and then you need a dedicated time frame in which to execute that plan. You work at your maximum when you are in the zone, totally focused on the task at hand. I want to recommend that you create exactly such a zone.

In his book *The Talent Code*, Daniel Coyle talks about three elements that are necessary for the development of talent:

1. Practice/repetition
2. Great coaching
3. Total concentration

It is this third element that I find fascinating. Total concentration is about getting deep within a practice zone, where the rest of the world is tuned out and I am solely focused on the immediate task at hand. Total concentration is about intensity and resolve. It is evidence of an unquestionable desire to be and do one's very best.

I like to think that all true professionals get into that zone. If I need a brain operation, total concentration would be high on my list of attributes for my surgeon. Race car drivers have the uncanny ability to stay in the total concentration zone for hours at a time. Want a picture of total concentration? Go find a tennis ball and a Labrador retriever.

FROM THE FIELD

The end result of the right mindset, planning, and execution is something quite worthwhile. "After 24-plus years I still believe deep down that I am doing a service. Every time a buyer signs I feel I've done a good thing."

THE LEAD CONVERSION HOUR

When it comes to sales follow-up, that zone is something I call the Lead Conversion Hour.

I am a staunch proponent of focusing on your follow-up in chunks of dedicated time rather than making one call now and another in a couple of hours. I recommend this strategy because so much of follow-up is about your mental approach, and it is simply too difficult to gear up mentally for every individual call. Better to get in the zone and stay in it.

> *If you don't have time to do it right, when will you have the time to do it over?*
>
> —JOHN WOODEN

This is the direct opposite of a strategy that could best be described as "winging it." Weaker salespeople stare at a list of names, phone numbers, and categorized tasks that are dictated by the CRM. The tasks are burdensome because they lack creativity, they are mundane, and they don't feel particularly useful.

The approach of the weak salesperson? Stare at the CRM, sigh, walk away, get a cup of coffee, check Facebook.

If you don't have both a system and a dedicated time frame in which to execute on that system, you are left with the winging-it approach.

Proper planning changes all that.

The Lead Conversion Hour is a dedicated and specific period of time that appears as a firm appointment on your calendar. It is "zone" time, and it requires your complete focus. No interruptions, no distractions, no excuses.

The Lead Conversion Hour is 60 minutes of single-mindedness. Nothing else exists except your undeniable thirst to get your prospects over the finish line. It's one hour of crushing your follow-up.

GET YOUR MINDSET RIGHT

Begin your Lead Conversion Hour with a five-minute prep session. That's it. Just five minutes of intensive planning will make all the difference in the world. In that time, you can ensure you are properly focused in two ways: mindset and execution.

When your follow-up time rolls around, your tendency will be to start by looking at your task list. I strongly recommend you begin instead by doing some mental prep. This will dramatically increase your effectiveness during your follow-up time.

Visualize Your Success

Take just a few moments to ensure you are playing offense and not defense. Feel what it will be like to add value, to have positive conversations, and to advance your prospects along in their buying journey. Get that sense in your gut that this is gonna be good!

Raise Your Confidence

Confidence is the sum of two components: belief and mastery. See yourself mastering the perfect follow-up call and believe that you are doing something truly valuable for your prospect. This is critical because confidence is contagious. You want your customer to adopt your confidence.

Elevate Your Emotional Altitude

You get to decide your own mental strength and your own Emotional Altitude. You can decide to be grumpy about follow-up, or you can decide to be excited about follow-up. Guess which approach the top professionals take?

Create Contagious Energy

Like confidence, the energy you bring into the conversation will be adopted by your customer. Come in with a boring and neutral tone, and your customer will follow your emotional lead. You don't have to be hyper, but you must be energetic. Ask yourself this question: Would I want my customer to adopt the energy level I have right now?

Adopt a "Show Time!" Mindset

Think of your prep work as a "backstage" process. Your customer does not see the work that goes on behind the curtain, but it is integral to the success of the show. Now think of the actual call as a "front stage" activity. It happens in full view of the prospect. Your follow-up cannot be seen as an administrative task. You are on the front stage, and this is show time!

Make it a habit. Always follow the same mental regimen for those five minutes at the start of your follow-up process.

My friend (and sales guru) Jill Konrath offers strong advice on how to maximize your follow-up approach: "To keep sales momentum alive, you need to provide value on every interaction—even a quick follow-up call."

PROCESS PLANNING

With your mindset ready for action, turn your attention to task planning. That process should consist of three steps that should take only a couple of minutes.

Set Goals

Begin with the end in mind. Think about what you want to accomplish by the end of the session. How many people do you want to reach? How much time are you allotting to this follow-up session? How many times will you ask for the order in the next 30 or 60 minutes? Who are your highest value targets?

When you take a moment to jot down your goals, you are far more likely to stay mentally strong just when Resistance comes along and tells you to have a cup of coffee and check Instagram rather than make another call.

Simplify Your Tasks

Most CRMs are extremely robust, with a seemingly endless list of tasks. Ignore everything that does not aid in your success during your lead conversion session. Spend just a few minutes looking at your goals and then determining what really matters. You don't need to study every detail of every contact; you need only to focus on what will advance your goals on this call.

Commit to Your Commitment

Your tendency will be to make a call and then take a break. Don't do it— you'll lose momentum. Instead, commit to following up nonstop through your lead conversion time. Have the calls lined up, and the moment you hang up with one prospect, immediately call another. Stay in the zone!

> *The only thing that is an inhibitor is not time, but rather allowing a bad behavior to creep in of not scheduling specific time for follow-up or lead conversion activities. If it's booked, it happens!*
>
> —JASON BURROWS

DANGERS

While you may be 100 percent committed to your Lead Conversion Hour and have the right mindset and the appropriate determination, beware the nuisances that will get in your way and make you less than effective.

Watch out for these three:

Complexity

Your goals for each call must be simple. If you add too many objectives, you will lose track mid-call of what you were trying to accomplish. What is the next logical step to advance this sale along? Focus on that.

Overplanning

Don't wait for the lights to all turn green before you leave the house. When you stare at a prospect's CRM entry for too long you lose some steam. Set the goal, make a plan, and dial the number. Don't get bogged down with minutia such that the quality of the call diminishes.

Distractions

It is always best to find a quiet place at an uninterrupted time. The world is full of disruptions; you must shield yourself from them. Turn off all unnecessary devices. Close web pages on your browser. Put up a sign for those around you. Close your blinds so you can't see squirrels. Do whatever you have to do to protect your focus.

EXPERT OPINION

B2B sales expert and author Jill Konrath shares three follow-up strategies that can replace "Just touching base."

1. Reemphasize the value.
2. Share ideas and insights.
3. Continue to educate.

THE CHALLENGE

Are you tired of slogging through your follow-up sessions? A little planning will go a long way. It's time to plan for your planning sessions.

Look back over the instructions in this chapter and write a plan for how you will approach your Lead Conversion Hour. Start with your mindset points, followed by your goal planning, and then your strategy for eliminating distractions.

Proper planning produces peak performance. Approach your follow-up sessions with preparation, with confidence, and with positive energy. Let's do it!

Self-Study Questions:

1. What are the distractions at work that keep you from doing follow-up? How would you clear these items from a portion of your day to be focused in the follow-up zone?

2. Remember that success in follow-up isn't always about the final sale. What are other elements of progress that you could visualize as coming from a follow-up action?

3. Think of two different current prospects. What could you do or say in a follow-up communication to reemphasize value, share ideas and insights, and continue to educate these individuals?

4. Have you ever put too much complexity into a follow-up communication? How could you pare that back to something realistic with an achievable goal?

5. Get in the zone and track your actual follow-up performance (e.g., number of calls, times asking for the order, total value of prospects contacted). How could you increase your performance by 10 percent?

Now Do This:

It's show time! Start your Lead Conversion Hour now! Visualize your success and make the calls . . . *now*. I mean it—really get going!

9

Selecting the Right Follow-Up Method

Not all follow-up is created equal; different situations call for different methods. The sales professional must think strategically in choosing which tool to use for which job.

THE PATH OF LEAST RESISTANCE

You wouldn't use a hammer when trying to unclog a toilet nor a plunger when trying to drive a nail. There are different tools for different jobs.

Need to confirm a follow-up appointment? A phone call could be obnoxious. Need to share some unpleasant news with a prospect? Stay away from text messaging.

Pick the method that best suits the situation.

> *We become what we behold. We shape our tools, and thereafter our tools shape us.*
>
> —MARSHALL MCLUHAN

Too many salespeople choose the communication method based upon their own personal comfort levels, rather than the most effective tool for the job.

For example, I find email to be a relatively simple, and therefore comfortable, form of communication. Let's say I have important information that solves a significant problem for a buyer. The easy way to communicate: send an email. "Good news! I have a solution for your concern about . . ."

But if, in this example, I am solving a major problem that makes it easier for the customer to move forward, wouldn't I want to be on the phone to ask for the sale immediately upon the resolution of said problem?

Are you selecting your follow-up medium based on what is easy for you or what is effective for your prospect?

> *With text messaging and emails buzzing in our pockets, our constant availability for phone calls, and hot new apps and social media on our phones, we are more distracted, more unfocused, and more enmeshed in sweating the small stuff than ever before. And this leads to many of us feeling like we're sprinting every day but really not getting anywhere.*
>
> —DEAN GRAZIOSI

Beware of your own tendencies, my friend. Our brains are designed for one primary function: to keep us alive, to survive. When you face a discomfort (making a phone call, for example), your brain has a tendency to interpret that discomfort as a threat. And when you feel threatened, your brain goes into survival mode.

Survival mode triggers a fight-or-flee option. Of those two choices, the option to flee tends to win out. When you find yourself in an uncomfortable situation your brain sends a message instructing you to bail out of the situation. To make things even easier, the brain offers some plausible alternative that will bring about a greater level of comfort.

In other words, if you want to win at sales there are times when you need to override the natural instincts of your brain. You must retrain your mind so that you can lean into your discomforts rather than bailing out. (For more on this phenomenon, pick up a copy of my book *Be Bold and Win the Sale*, a book dedicated to overcoming comfort addictions in sales.)

THE DANGEROUS COMFORTABLE CHOICE

With an understanding of how the brain works, we can easily see how we can get fooled into believing that the most comfortable way to follow up is also the best way. That explains why emails are sent when phone calls are more appropriate, or text messages are delivered when video messages would have far greater impact.

In every case ask yourself the critical question: What is in the *customer's* best interest? Do not answer this question according to your personal preference. Having answered the question, ask one more: Did I just rationalize the answer because I'm uncomfortable?

> Don't assume the medium you're most comfortable with is the same communication medium your buyer prefers. I have some buyers who return texts in minutes, while other clearly have twitter alerts on their phone. Recently I've been using Facebook chat to talk to buyers as well.
>
> —JAMIE SHANKS

Suppose you were working with a prospect who had to make a difficult decision about spending much more than he had previously considered. He sees the potential benefits, so this would not be classified as a value perception problem. Rather, he has a price-paradigm problem; he did not enter the buying process thinking he would spend as much as he will need to.

Further suppose that you had a past client who had gone through the exact same deliberation before coming to the right conclusion. How valuable would it be for your current prospect to hear from your past client, someone who had already been through the same dilemma and had chosen to move forward?

In this example, recording a video testimonial from your past client could be an incredibly powerful option for advancing the sale, yes? But asking that past client to be interviewed on camera for 60 seconds is well outside your comfort zone.

Enter the rationalizations as to why you should *not* make that request. I mean, will the new prospect really be all that impressed? And isn't the speed of a text more important than the time it would take? And can I do something that looks good from my smartphone? And do I really want to do this when Jupiter is in Libra? (Trust me. We can get really creative when it comes to fabricating rationalization stories.)

THE COMMUNICATION HIERARCHY

So how does one choose which method to utilize? The only way to do that is to consider the impact on the customer. What resonates? What triggers the emotional impulse? What connects most deeply?

Consider this sequence of the most-to-least effective forms of communication:

Face to Face

Our brains are wired for face-to-face interaction. We commit a whole lot of brainpower to reading the face and facial expressions of others. That diminishes dramatically when we use any other method. Albert Mehrabian's landmark book *Silent Messages* indicates the greater importance of facial expression and tone of voice over words alone when it comes to the communications of feelings.

Voice to Voice

Even though we lose the visual impact of a face-to-face conversation we can still send important inflection and emphasis cues over the phone. Our voice carries with it a degree of energy that is easily adopted by a prospect. Written messages tend to lack the emotion necessary to propel a prospect along in the buying journey, whereas verbal messages communicate emotion above everything else.

Personalized Video

Downside: One-way communication. Upside: You can prove your dedication while standing out from the crowd. You can still communicate energy, enthusiasm, and emotion even if you are not in a two-way conversation. And good news: Video is still a novel method of follow-up. When was the last time you received a personalized video follow-up from a salesperson? (I rest my case.)

Voice to Voice Mail

You miss out on the give-and-take of a two-way conversation, but you can still communicate energy, optimism, and urgency in a voice-mail message. The key here is to make sure your voice mail includes a specific call to action. There must be a reason for a customer to return your call. "Hi, I'm just checking in . . ." isn't gonna do it.

Personalized Email

There is a place for this, especially as a way to send dense information quickly. But don't call it communication; the root of that word implies a two-way exchange. Far too many salespeople send a prewritten, highly formulated email and call it follow-up. Nope. That is nothing more than fodder for the virtual trash can.

Text Message

We diminish just about all of the human connection when we rely on text messaging. And please don't tell me that emojis, GIFs, and memes accurately take the place of human interaction. Is there a place for texting in follow-up? Yes, there is. But it is a supplemental tool, not a primary tool.

FROM THE FIELD

We asked our survey group what percentage of their follow-up is done by different means. Here are the results:

- Email: 38 percent
- Phone: 34 percent
- Text: 19 percent
- Face to face: 13 percent
- Video: 5 percent
- Social media: 3 percent

SELECTING THE METHOD

Let me offer some very top-level rules of thumb for your consideration. This isn't set in stone, but it provides a starting point for your communication decision.

Use the Telephone For . . .

Sharing exciting and/or important news. You want to communicate your enthusiasm and encourage your prospect to enjoy the moment. This is difficult to do in any other way.

Extending the relationship. Healthy relationships are based on healthy and heartfelt communication. There are nuances in the voice-to-voice conversation that simply cannot be relayed in an email or text message.

Conveying a message that requires a response. Every follow-up conversation should include a call to action. Preferably that action would be a purchase decision, but there must be some next step. You don't want to put your customer in a position to own that next move. You want to ask directly to confirm the next action while customers are still on the phone.

Closing. Yes, I do believe it is appropriate to ask for a commitment over the telephone once the standing issues have been resolved. This does not require some special technique; you can ask the same way you would if the customer were standing in front of you. Go for it!

Use Video For . . .

Introducing yourself before an appointment. Not technically a follow-up moment, but call it a pre-follow-up. That brief introductory video proves that you are a kind person and that you are sincerely interested in serving. This goes a long way toward reducing any pre-meeting anxieties and allows you to develop a relationship much more quickly.

Showing features or lifestyle opportunities. Video paints such a vivid picture of what the future could look like. Send videos that show future enjoyment. Raise the emotion level!

Use Email For . . .

Sending dense information. Email is great for sending reports or other forms of extended data. However, be sure to send that information as an attachment rather than a 12-paragraph wall of text. Assume a short attention span. And be sure to end with a confirmation on the next step in the process.

Handling administrative tasks. In many sales transactions there are several steps in order to complete a formal purchase (financing approval, selection of options, etc.). Email works great for those kinds of tasks.

Sending multiple large photos. No doubt about it. Attach a photo and you increase the open rate by 80 percent.[1] Further, photos represent such compelling visual interest as to increase the emotional involvement of the prospect. There are technical caveats: check with your IT department.

Sending videos. I'll talk more about this in Chapter 13, but make no mistake—personalized video messages are a *huge* boost to follow-up effectiveness.

Use Text Messaging For . . .

Confirming appointments. Keep it very brief. Just a quick note with the specifics. I would suggest you end that note with, "Does that work for you?" If you ask for confirmation, you increase the commitment level.

Very brief thank-you notes. This is particularly powerful as a follow-up to an initial presentation. Customers honored you with their time and attention; honor them with a thank you.

Sending one or two smaller photos. Use text messaging for a quick photo or two to emphasize a key point. Text may even be a more powerful medium for photos than email, especially when there is a specific issue you are trying to address or feature you are trying to highlight.

Sending short videos. Remember that people open texts more frequently than they open email. So if you record and send a short, personalized video, text messaging might be the right way to do that.

NOT SURE? ASK THE CUSTOMER

It is always a good idea to ask customers directly for their preferred communication method. However, don't get yourself locked into that. Give yourself some options.

SALESPERSON: "There are times I will need to call, and other times I will need to email. But what is your preferred method of communication?"

BUYER: "Well, I often don't answer the phone and I get a ton of email, so maybe texting is the best way to reach me."

SALESPERSON: "Fair enough. I'll try to use that as a primary option, unless the issue requires a deeper discussion. Then I'll call instead. Does that work?"

FROM THE FIELD

In our survey we asked folks to tell us their number-one best follow-up practice. Here's what one top sales pro said: "When I ask a customer or potential client the best way for me to communicate with them. It allows me to get their permission to follow up, and they'll often tell me the best medium to use to reach them."

CHALLENGE

This week, apply this communication hierarchy to an active prospect. Use the right method for the situation and track your results. I think you will find that your conversion rates increase when you think methodically about which method goes with which situation.

Let me also challenge you to do something uncomfortable in your follow-up efforts this week. Make a phone call when you would rather send an email. Send a video text message instead of a text-based message. Experiment. Have some fun. Stretch yourself.

Self-Study Questions:

1. Do an honest self-assessment. Which method of follow-up communication are you most comfortable with? Which are you least comfortable with?

2. When was the last time you sent a thank you note to a customer *before* closing a sale? Challenge yourself to do so five times in the next day. (Text message is OK! It only takes two minutes.)

3. How can changing up your method of follow-up communication be fun, even when it might make you uncomfortable?

4. If you ask your customers what method of communication they prefer, how will you keep track of this for each customer?

Now Do This:

Think of five customers you need to follow up with. For each, identify which method would be best *for the customer*, not for you, for the next follow-up step. Then do it.

10

Phone Follow-Up

*Would you like a precise and specific execution
of a truly great call? Use this framework to
design your perfect phone follow-up.*

THREE SIMPLE TRUTHS ABOUT THE TELEPHONE

What is old is new again. Discarded by sales practitioners everywhere, the telephone might just be your secret weapon. Here's why.

Truth #1: Voice-to-Voice Communication Trumps Everything but Face-to-Face Communication

We communicate best when we communicate completely. The problem with text, email, social messaging, etc., is that it is:

- One-sided

- Lacking the nuances we get in voice-to-voice communication

Suppose you were to send me a text message with the request, "I've got some exciting things to share about our new product. Call me!"

Now, you might indeed have some very exciting things to share, but what did I just hear? I heard, "This person wants to sell me something."

But suppose you called me and said, "Jeff, this is Janet over at _____. I was thinking about your specific situation regarding _____, and I've been doing some research; I think I can help with a solution. Do you have 30 seconds to chat?"

What did I, the prospect, just hear? I heard that:

- You were thinking about my problem.
- You heard me.
- You can help.
- This won't take long.

But more important, I heard your tone, your energy, your confidence, and your urgency. Assuming you had already earned my trust, I'm feeling pretty good about this call!

What's more, I could easily ignore your email or your text message, but you just made me a pretty compelling offer: 30 seconds of my time in exchange for a solution to my problem. That's a good deal!

Truth #2: Telephobia Is a "Thing"—Get over It

I know you might not love making phone calls. True confession time: I don't either. I admit to a natural discomfort with the telephone.

Social psychologists call this telephobia, defined as reluctance or fear of making or taking phone calls, literally, "fear of telephones." It is considered to be a type of social phobia or social anxiety.

Here is a different way to look at it. Just as I have a discomfort with telephones, I also have a discomfort with heights. But suppose my child was in a perilous position in a high place and needed to be rescued.

Would I save her? In a heartbeat! And why? Because she means that much to me.

And that's my point. I don't love the telephone, but I make and receive scores of phone calls every week. Why? Because the relationship with that other person is more important than my personal comfort level.

You're uncomfortable with the phone? Fine. You have permission to feel awkward. But you do *not* have permission to underserve your customers, not if you truly want to help them!

FROM THE FIELD

Our survey asked, "What keeps you from doing follow-up?" It might be surprising that not just 1 or 2 but 11 percent of our respondents said, "Telephobia." That's one in nine folks with a fear of or discomfort making a call, and these are salespeople whose jobs depend on reaching out to customers!

Truth #3: The More You Procrastinate, the Less Likely It Is That You Will Make a Call

Just make the call! Pick up the phone, dial the number, and talk to the nice people on the other end of the line.

What's the worst thing that could happen? Seriously, what is the worst-case scenario? Physical assault? Probably not. A lawsuit? Unlikely. The *worst* case is probably a stern rejection, but if you did your job properly in the first place and if you have something useful to bring to the conversation, that scenario is highly unlikely.

Make the stinking phone call!

The telephone is the greatest nuisance among conveniences, the greatest convenience among nuisances.

—ROBERT STAUGHTON LYND

> *The most difficult thing is the decision to act,*
> *the rest is merely tenacity. The fears are paper*
> *tigers. You can do anything you decide to do.*
> *You can act to change and control your life; and*
> *the procedure, the process is its own reward.*
>
> —AMELIA EARHART

THE TELEPHONE: WHY IT STILL WORKS

The way we use our phones has changed (from landlines to cell phones), but the amount of usage has remained consistent. It's just that now people are imminently more reachable.[1]

Of course, that constant access to our cell phones has brought with it the dreaded robocalls and other such spam that sometimes make us cringe when we hear our ringer. Though the numbers are trending down, Americans receive 26 billion robocalls per year.[2]

Consequently, too many sales practitioners are worried that they will be lumped in with telemarketers and other annoyances of life. We work off our firsthand experience, and we know how much we hate spam calls.

Can I ask you to keep something in mind? That is not *you*! You are not lumped in with robocalls and telemarketers. The difference? You've built a relationship with the people you're calling. They already know who you are, and, presumably, they already like you.

Too many salespeople are using other methods for their follow-up efforts (email, text messaging, social media). To me, that smells like opportunity. I want to zig when others zag. I want to do things others won't do in order to achieve results they won't even dream of.

PREPARING FOR YOUR CALLS

A few things to keep in mind if you want to make a truly great call:

1. *Your comfort—or discomfort—is contagious.*
   If you are uncomfortable, you will quickly and effortlessly pass that discomfort on to your prospect. But think about it. There is no reason to be uncomfortable. You are simply extending the existing relationship. This should be fun!

2. *Warm up through repetition.*
   Practice your opening lines a few times. Think like an actress or a musician. Get into the role. It will only take a few moments, and it will help you mentally prepare to be fully on your game.

3. *Determine the primary purpose of your call before you dial.*
   This will always come down to one of three reasons for making the call. Go through the checklist before you pick up the phone.

   - What value will you add?
   - What problem will you solve?
   - What question will you answer?

Prepare some bullet points. I'm not a huge fan of reading scripts because your customers can *always* tell when they are being read to. But I am a fan of having strategy points written out. What are the key points to communicate? Jot them down in advance.

Determine the urgency message of your call. Why should your customer respond today? What is the "right now" message? Don't fall into the bad habit of simply sharing information and waiting for your customer to ask permission to buy. Tell customers why it is in their best interest to act today.

Want to get this down solid? Practice with a friend. Just follow that same pre-call pattern before you make the call and see how much better it goes.

"My passion for follow-up started almost immediately in my sales career because I found this to be the niche that set me apart from all the others. Ninety-five percent of the people I competed with just didn't do this. I knew that if I treated my customers well, shared good information with them, and left a reason to call, they would welcome my call. So one trick learned early, have an agreed-upon reason and time for the call. The call should never be a surprise."

CONTROLLING YOUR ENVIRONMENT

Like a physician in an operating room of a hospital, you want to create an environment that will allow for success. Be intentional about this. Setting the stage goes a long way to making certain you can play the part effectively. That means:

- Get rid of all distractions: Facebook, email, messy desks, irritating people, etc. Find a place where you can tune out the rest of the world.

- Commit to 100 percent focus. Make an agreement with yourself to be totally present in these calls.

- Set the goal before you dial. What is the best possible outcome? If you can't land the sale, what is the next best outcome?

- Have your notes handy so you can refer back to them to make a personal connection.

- Create positive energy. If your call time starts at 10 a.m., feel free to put on the headphones at 9:55 and rock out for five minutes. "Eye of the Tiger," "Start Me Up," "Beautiful Day"—they all work. Better yet, try Blondie's "Call Me!"

CLARIFYING YOUR STRATEGIC OBJECTIVES

Your calls will be far more effective if you follow a simple, three-step strategy: connect, advance, close.

Strategic Objective #1: Connect

Pick up where the relationship left off. If you are responding quickly enough, you are simply extending the previous conversation and assuming a strong personal connection.

Strategic Objective #2: Advance

Add value. Think through how you will make this person's life better as a result of the value you are about to bring.

Strategic Objective #3: Close

Ask for a new commitment (final or next step). Yes, you can do this on the phone!

CREATING YOUR PROCESS

Here's an example of what I believe to be a simple and highly effective 10-step process for completing a great follow-up call:

1. Clear your mind (and your desk).
2. Smile before you dial.
3. Identify yourself right away.
4. Refresh the relationship. Pick a personal connection point.
5. Get to the purpose of your call as soon as possible.

6. Add value by providing a service (give).

7. Ask a temperature close question (ask).

8. Get to your objective (close, second appointment, etc.).

9. Agree on the next step.

10. End on a positive and happy note.

LEAVING A VOICE MAIL

Voice-to-voice is hands-down the most effective manner of communication. Therefore, I recommend not leaving a voice mail until your third attempt at a voice-to-voice call.

A voice mail requires that the prospect take further action (return the call), which places you out of control of the conversation. You want the burden of action to be on you, not on the prospect.

When you do leave a voice mail, let prospects know that you have something they want. But keep it brief; long-winded voice mails are wearisome. Be prepared to leave a voice mail anytime you place a call. Make sure your first 10 words are high value so recipients don't click delete.

ADAPTING TO CURVEBALLS

Of course, not every call will go as swimmingly as you hope it will. Sometimes you have to adjust quickly when it doesn't seem to be headed in the right direction.

Rudeness

Could it happen? Yes, it could. You might end up with someone who is legitimately annoyed that you called.

Here is something to keep in mind: You don't know what's going on in the person's life. And you certainly don't know what is going on in that moment of the day. Sometimes a call comes at exactly the wrong time. We've all been there.

Think like a counselor, and don't overrespond to negative attitudes. Simply apologize, let prospects know you have something they want, and ask for the right time to call back.

Objections

The best way to understand a prospect's objection is to realize that there is always a gap between what prospects want and what they perceive you are offering. In that gap lies the objection.

Because there is no such thing as a perfect solution, there will always be objections. Keep this in mind, however: If the objection was a deal-killer, they wouldn't be talking to you. The fact that they are sharing the objection means that your solution, while not perfect, is still in play.

The process is no different than what we've always been taught in sales:

- Thank prospects for their honesty and clarity.
- Ask for greater clarification: "Tell me more."
- Answer the objection.
- Close if you can.

Rejection

Of course, there are times when a customer will flat out decide that it's over. The decision has been made, and it is final.

But before you throw in the towel, there is one more question that can yet be asked: "Are you saying 'not now' or 'not ever'?"

Sometimes it's a matter of timing. The prospect still has a problem that needs to be solved, but the timing just doesn't work at present. That's why the "not yet" inquiry is so powerful.

GETTING TO WORK

OK, you've got the background, the data, the mindset, and the process. Now make the call! Don't sit around and think about it. Don't overplan. Success goes to those who take action.

That phone call you haven't made yet because you're uncomfortable? Follow the 10-step process and *make the call!*

Self-Study Questions:

1. What is your level of telephobia? Have you ever *not* made a phone call you should have because of discomfort?

2. Think of the worst follow-up phone call you've ever had. What were the unhappy consequences? You survived, didn't you?

3. Jot down your memory of the 10-step process. Which steps did you miss? Go back and review. Make sure you include all 10 steps in your own process going forward.

4. How does smiling while talking on the phone help to ensure positive communication and especially a positive start and end? (Try a few calls in front of the mirror and check your facial expression.)

5. What is your value-adding first line if you need to leave a voice message?

Now Do This:

Write down the name of a person you know you need to call. Refer back to the 10-step process for creating a great call. Now do it! Make the call!

11

Email Follow-Up

*Email can be a powerful follow-up tool
or a colossal waste of time. Learning how
and when to use email successfully will
help you shorten the buying cycle.*

EMAIL HISTORY

In the early 1990s, the options available to send clients reports, data, and various bits of useful information were limited. Basically, you could send via costly overnight courier or deal with messy and difficult-to-read fax transmissions.

Along came email, swooping in like a hero with a cape. Email allowed us to dramatically increase the speed of communication, even if it meant waiting for our dial-up modem to connect. We could send quick notes and provide important information at the touch of a button.

Can you recall the early days of email? Specifically, the disjointed melody of an AOL connection, complete with the dial tone, the song of a ringing phone, the clicking of a connection, the shrill sound of data reaching data, and the satisfying confirmation that you had access to the World Wide Web. (I'm . . . uh . . . dating myself here.)

At any rate, once connected, we were thrilled with the charming and chipper voice of a polite gentleman lyrically announcing, "You've got mail!"

We loved email . . . until we hated it.

> *It's quicker, easier, and involves less licking.*
>
> —Douglas Adams

We failed to recognize that email was a Trojan horse, and lurking inside was a monster that went by the name of Time Suck. In short order we enslaved ourselves to a seemingly endless flow of communication, most of it unwanted.

THE NUMBERS ON EMAIL

The average daily global *legitimate* email volume currently comes in at 53.65 billion.[1] Wow!

But think about this: The average daily global *spam* email volume is 302.99 billion. Double wow!

Only about 15 percent of email is legit. The rest, 85 percent, is pure garbage.

The amount of flat-out abuse via email is staggering, from phishing scams to unwanted political articles sent by relatives to promising opportunities from Nigerian princes. Email went from a helpful tool to a hated adversary.

As a reaction, we've thrown the baby out with the bathwater. As a society, we have learned how to tune out email and ignore its content.

Over time we have invented various tactics to deal with this incessant beast.

Our email filters try to spot spam and reject it. If the sender address is "no-reply@ . . ." or something weird (e.g., gvt43020@t2221q.ml), the email is likely to go to Never Neverland, even if it is legit.

Spammy words in the subject line are also likely to get an email sent to a junk folder without the recipient ever knowing it's been sent. Trigger words like "free," "buy now," "act today," "no gimmicks," and "one-time only" will destine the message to the electronic wasteland. Exclamation points, asterisks, or all caps are also common spam indicators.

Those filters take care of a lot of known junk, but unwanted email still gets through.

THE MOST COMMON EMAIL TACTIC: IGNORE

In need of a strategy to deal with the Time Suck monster, we adopt an entirely effective process; it's called "ignore."

The ignoring of emails is a tactic so widely used that we have grown to accept it as a normal practice. How many times have you heard (or . . . ahem . . . said) the words, "I never got that email"?

I confess that when I am checking my own emails I am doing so with one finger on the delete button at all times. In fact, I cannot delete emails quickly enough.

Why the great love for the delete button? Because if we were to get our heads around the sheer number of emails we receive each day, if we really wanted to scrutinize the potential value in each email, we would need to be prepared to part with two valuable commodities: attention and time. As it stands, we are woefully short of available attention, and discretionary time is a concept we can only vaguely recall from our childhood.

Think of attention as currency (hence the request to "*pay* attention"). Your customer is already overwhelmed with the various inputs of everyday life. To pay out some of their valuable currency attention for each email received is asking an awful lot.

I don't think we are any different than our customers. We cannot possibly pay attention to each email we receive. Why do we think our customers can do it?

SO WHERE ARE WE?

We are left with the conclusion that:

- Email is commonly abused.

- People regularly ignore emails they receive.

- Salespeople add to the problem by emailing when a different communication method might be more appropriate.

Sounds like it's time to scrap the use of email altogether, right? Not so fast. Email can still play an invaluable role in follow-up—if you learn how to use it properly. That means getting your email opened by the customer and getting it read.

In fact, email returns per dollar spent are significantly higher than for mobile marketing, social media, display ads, and search engine marketing.[2]

TO OPEN, OR NOT TO OPEN

Deciding on the proper use of email begins with answering an important question: Which emails get opened, and which get deleted? After all, it doesn't matter how strong the content is if no one ever sees it, right?

Across all industries, the average email open rate is 15 to 25 percent,[3] roughly 2 out of 10. That might seem like a low number, but when I think about my own itchy delete finger, it sounds about right.

So, if you can get just one more email out of 10 opened and read? That's a 50 percent increase in opportunities!

What is your email open rate? Do you know how to track it?

How do customers decide which emails to open and which to delete? Look at the following triggers:

Positive Triggers

- Known sender and sender name. The better your relationship, the more likely the email will be opened.

- Effective subject line. Short subject lines are most successful.

- Personalized, with your customer's name in the subject line.

- Images, but not too many. Too big a file and an IT department will block it.

- Appealing first line and paragraph. For many email platforms the reader can see the subject line and the first words of the body text at the same time.

- Excellent content. If you don't have excellent content, it deserves to be deleted.

Negative Triggers

- Spammy subject line. You are asking for the message to get sent right to the junk folder.

- Unidentified or unfamiliar sender.

- Spelling errors, typos, etc.

- Not optimized for mobile. At the time of this writing, 55 percent of emails are opened on mobile devices.[4]

- Wall of text. It's just obnoxious. Keep it brief!

FROM THE FIELD

"Sometimes you have information to share with the prospect that is more lengthy in nature and doesn't lend itself to text. I like to call or text the prospect and tell them I'm sending an important email right before I send it. The response rate is extremely high compared to just sending an email or trying to send too much information via text."

THE FIRST LINE COUNTS!

How does the first line impact open rate? Many people screen emails without even opening them by having their inbox set up with a split screen for previews. If a quick scan of the visible part of the body is appealing enough, they click "open" on the message rather than "delete." Great first lines and images help . . . a lot!

Folks who use their cell phones for email see the sender, the subject, the date . . . and *the very first sentence of the body*. Talk about the perfect opportunity to catch recipients' attention before they swipe left and delete!

But the first line should count for you as well. Ask yourself an important question: Does this message add value? If you cannot add value in the first sentence, rethink whether you want to send it at all.

Don't forget personalization. Outreach manager Sam Nelson observes that "personalizing just the first two sentences of an email can deliver a dramatic increase in open rates." Even if you're reusing content from one customer to another later in the body—and that is often helpful for productivity—make the first line or two about just the one person in the "To" line.

THE BOTTOM LINE ON EMAIL

Despite the lack of facial and tone-of-voice expression, despite the high incidence of spam, despite the fact that millennials seem to stick up their noses at anything but text and tweets, email still serves a great purpose. Even young consumers prefer email for business communications.[5] It's hard to beat.

THE GOLDEN RULE

Before you send that next follow-up email to a prospect, consider asking yourself: Would you open and read it if you were the receiver? And would you be really pleased if you did?

That simple test will go a very long way toward determining whether you are adding value or just adding to the noise.

Self-Study Questions:

1. Check the first 20 emails in your inbox. How many reach out to you to be opened? What are the positive triggers that make you want to open them?

2. Look at 20 emails in your inbox *on your cellphone*. How many have visible personalization and catchy content?

3. Check the first 20 emails in your sent folder. How many deserve to be opened? How would you increase the positive triggers and decrease the negative triggers?

4. If you have already attached a photo or video to a customer follow-up email, great. If not, practice doing it now so you know how to make it work. Send to yourself, your spouse, a friend. Check to be sure that it looks OK and works well, even on mobile.

Now Do This:

Pick a customer you need to follow up with by email. Write the most personalized "open me now" email you've ever written. There! Didn't that feel good?

Get into the habit of asking yourself: Would I open and read it if I were the receiver? And would I be pleased if I did?

12

Text Message Follow-Up

The immediacy of texting makes it an outstanding follow-up tool. The annoyance of texting makes it dangerous. Use it wisely and you're golden. Use it foolishly and it will cost you sales!

A NEW COMMUNICATIONS OPPORTUNITY

At the turn of the century we barely knew what texting was. And those who understood the technology at all had to become proficient at the good old multi-tap (tapping keys repeatedly until the desired letter came up). For most, sending a text message was laborious and inefficient.

Still, the technology had its advantages, particularly for those who just didn't like making phone calls. Texting gained momentum throughout the early years of the century.

Two events occurred in 2007. First, Apple introduced the iPhone, complete with touch screen capability. That phone launched a tidal wave of change in the world of communication.

The second was directly connected to that launch: For the first time, people sent and received more text messages per month than phone calls.

The world of communications would never be the same.

SO WHERE ARE WE TODAY?

Check out the stats:[1]

- Americans send 26 billion text messages a day!
- Texting is the single most common usage for smartphones.
- 97 percent of smartphone users text regularly.
- According to a 2012 report, more people around the world text than have electricity in their homes.
- On average, Americans send and receive 94 text messages per day.
- Americans spend twice as much time texting as using email.

I'm going to go out on a limb here and predict that texting is here to stay! At least until we all receive neural implants that allow us to send messages cybernetically with our thoughts.

THE UPSIDE OF TEXTING

Texting is universally popular for good reason:

Texting Offers Fast Communication

In a society that cherishes and rewards speed, texting is an awesome tool. We can send and receive information in the blink of an eye. We can stay visible with a single emoticon. We can confirm an appointment with a single tap. We can make someone smile with a well-picked GIF.

Small data can travel quickly and efficiently.

Texting Increases Touch Points

I love the people in my life, but I don't want to have a conversation about every two-bit issue or task that comes along. Texting allows me a quick and painless way to stay continually connected.

Texts Get Read

According to *Mobile Marketing Watch*, 98 percent of all text messages are opened compared to just 22 percent of emails.[2]

AND THE DOWNSIDE?

Alas, the overdependency on texting as a primary form of communication might be doing significant damage to your relationship with your prospect. Watch out for these traps.

Texting Is One-Way Communication

Texting is not an effective dialogue; it is a series of very small monologues, often disconnected over time. We sometimes lose context and meaning when we rely too much on texting. The endless back-and-forth can become exceedingly annoying.

It's Difficult to Share or Detect Emotion via Text

One of the key benefits of voice-to-voice communication is the expression of emotion. In a conversation it's not just the words we use; it is the inflection that makes all the difference. How many times have we been burned because a text message did not convey the intended emotion?

Texts Get Lost in the Noise of Other Texts

Picture yourself receiving a text, taking a quick glance, and then saying to yourself, "I'll respond to that later." What happens next? That text gets buried under 15 other messages. The fact is that it is far too easy to ignore a text message. (At least it is for me!)

Texting Hinders Relational Depth

Texting is easy, but it can be seen as a lazy alternative to a phone call. Relationships take time and effort and emotion, but mostly they take an abundance of two-way communication. The ease of texting does nothing to deepen that human connection.

> *Any text is the result of a repertoire, on conscious and unconscious levels, and can only be decoded by someone privy to the same repertoire.*
>
> —IVAN ANGELO

MEETING CUSTOMERS WHERE THEY ARE

The fact is that we are part of a world that places a very high premium on speed. We want fast food, fast cars, fast delivery (thanks, Amazon!), and fast information.

I was recently measured for a custom-made shirt from a large national men's clothing retailer. No sooner had I walked out the door than I received a text message thanking me for the order and providing a website URL if I needed assistance. A week later I received a follow-up text with a different URL so I could track the shipping progress. Finally, I received a text message the day after delivery asking for confirmation that I had received the shirt and including a URL in case I had any issues or concerns.

That was all through an automated system, and it was all very much appreciated. Quick, easy, effective.

What does this have to do with your own text messaging practices? Plenty. The fact is that automated systems like the one I just described are actually training consumers to appreciate text messages that are concise, helpful, and timely. Customers don't care whether they come from people or from bots; *their only concern is whether the text adds value.*

So that's the million-dollar question. Do your text messages add value? Because if they do not, you are wasting your customers' valuable attention on something that brings only annoyance.

THE CASE FOR FOLLOW-UP TEXTING

So, the question is asked: To text or not to text as a means of following up with a prospect?

And the answer is . . . it depends. Without question there is a place for texting in sales. Look at this recent data:

- 90 percent of people say they'd rather receive a text than a phone call from a business.[3]

- 95 percent of texts from businesses are read within three minutes of being sent.[4]

That is a pretty compelling argument based on customer preferences. Let's go on the assumption that texting, when done right, enhances the buying experience.

Suppose you are selling pleasure boats, a truly discretionary purchase. You are working with a prospect who is torn between buying something new—at considerably more cost—or going with the cheaper but riskier route and buying used. His last comment to the sales rep: "I need to spend some time doing comparison shopping and seeing what I can find."

What would a bad follow-up text look like? Something like this:

"I hope you buy from us. We would love your business."

What a colossal waste of time and energy! Of course you would love this guy's business. You get paid when you get his business. It's your job to get his business.

FROM THE FIELD

"I've been relentless in reaching out despite unreturned calls/texts/ emails. I finally got someone to respond to my text after months and months of reaching out. He was going through a challenging time in his life, soon to be divorced and the timing wasn't right for him to respond to me until now. He ended up buying a home! Never give up."

Here are five examples of appropriate text messages:

1. "Great chatting with you, Richard. Let me do some research for you. I'll call you at 5:00 with more information about . . ."

2. "I came across this really helpful article about deciding between a new and a used boat—a very balanced opinion (include link). I'll call you tomorrow."

3. "Here are three pictures of the Raptor model you're looking at. Good-looking boat, my friend!" (include photos).

4. Send a video walk-around of the exact boat he is looking at. Narrate it according to what is important to this buyer.

5. "I found this article that talks about the dependability of our line of boats. Definitely something to consider if you're also thinking about buying used."

In each case your objective is to sustain that Emotional Altitude. Keep your customer emotionally engaged.

TWO WORDS OF WARNING

First, let me encourage you to think about this subject not from your own perspective but from the perspective of your customer. We all have our ideas and preferences when it comes to texting, but for our purposes the only thing that matters is the customer's preference.

There is a significant difference between social texting and sales texting. Social texting carries an implied informality. Typos are easily forgiven. Emojis serve as a quick alternative to typing out a message. In the sales process, such informality is risky. It is best not to assume that level of casualness.

Second, you must not allow your own desire for comfort to dictate the method by which you follow up. Many salespeople follow up by text not because it is the most effective method but because it is the most comfortable method.

Texting must not become a crutch to be relied upon because of its ease of use. Voice-to-voice conversations are always more effective in continuing the relationship with a prospect. Do not fall into the assumption that your customer would prefer a text when, if you're being honest, you are simply following your own preference.

It's good to think about texting in the context of your overall follow-up communications strategy. A recent Velocify study found that customers who were sent text messages only *after* initial contact had been made in some other way converted at more than twice the rate of the average contacted lead.[5]

TEXTING DOS

- Ask for permission.
- Keep your texts positive.
- Complete your words. (No LOLs or IMHOs.)
- Check your spelling, especially because of autocorrect.
- Be brief. One sentence is best. Two max.
- Be professional.

TEXTING DON'TS

- Don't get cute; it can be misinterpreted.
- Don't text after hours without permission.
- Don't use jargon and acronyms.
- Don't let a text conversation go on too long. (Pick up the phone!)
- Don't bombard the customer. Some people still pay per-text rates.

One other important don't: If you are in a live, face-to-face conversation with a prospect, you should never have your cell phone out. The temptation of a quick glance when a new text message comes in is just too great. Even if your phone is on silent, the buzzing of a new text message will register in your brain and cause you to shift attention from the person in front of you. Don't be a slave to your text messages!

> *Cellaholics are those who interrupt quality time when they are with you, but rather text, call, and email others who are somewhere else.*
> —JAYCE O'NEAL

BEST PRACTICES FROM THE FIELD

I recently did an informal poll of sales professionals via LinkedIn, asking the following question: How do you use text messaging in your sales follow-up efforts (after an initial conversation but before you have a commitment)?

Here are some of the (rather interesting) responses:

- "I always ask their preference for follow-up: phone, email, or text. More people are opting for text messaging, and I find that the response time is quicker."

- "I offer to text a piece of helpful information to them before hanging up. Later, I reference the info sent and ask them another question. Works like a charm to keep the conversation going."

- "According to a friend in the text marketing business, people read text on average in four minutes. Virtually anything you send them will be read quickly . . . but it needs to add value to get a response."

- "On the initial interaction, I follow up merely to get in their phone. The platform I utilize has a drip campaign I will launch in the future, but only after I figure out a safe strategy. It is also noteworthy that this platform utilizes my actual mobile number, not a 'short code' as I feel these start the experience as being disingenuous."

- (From a homebuilder sales rep) "We utilize video follow-up texting so much! Short video of the kitchen the customer loved, community event with a homeowner testimonial, telling the customer about new pricing . . . We have had great response with this!"

- "I use texting to say thank-you, answer a question, provide additional information, confirm an appointment, and send a video update. It's rare that I won't get a response."

THE BOTTOM LINE ON TEXTING

Is there a place for texting? You bet. Is there an abuse of texting? Most definitely. The reality is that texting is here to stay; it is part of the fabric of the business world. Your task is to maximize effectiveness and minimize annoyance. Find the sweet spot and advance the sale!

Self-Study Questions:

1. What was the worst texting fail you've ever committed? Offending the receiver? Giving confusing information? Sending to the wrong person? Jot it down . . . and don't do it again!

2. It's possible to use as many as 918 characters for single texts. (It may be sent as separate sections stitched together.) Why is that much info in a text a bad idea for customer follow-up?

3. What are some potential problems with sending a text to customers without first talking to them on the phone?

4. When "asking permission," you'll probably find out individual customers have very different preferences for the timing of text messages. How will you manage all that information to avoid annoying them?

5. What will you do if you get a text response that sounds like the customer is upset?

Now Do This:

Go back and look at the last 5 to 10 texts that you sent to prospects. Analyze the content of the text and determine if you violated any of the texting rules from this chapter. Then ask yourself the all-important question: Did this text add value to the prospect?

It's show time again! Pick five customers who would be appropriate to text given where they are in the sales process. Follow the dos and don'ts and fire off those texts . . . *now*!

13

Video Follow-Up

Want to really stand out? Try doing what others aren't. Video follow-up is the secret weapon for making a huge and lasting impression.

WHY VIDEO?

If you were creating a dream sales impact tool, what would that look like?

- Exceedingly easy to execute
- Zero cost
- Huge impact
- Emotional engagement
- Fun

Ladies and gentlemen, meet video follow-up: the one form of communication that offers the highest-lasting impact for the least amount of effort.

CASE STUDY

Blake sells new homes in Austin, Texas. He received a call from a prospect who was most insistent that she wanted a large and wooded homesite.

If Blake could not offer that at his community she would look elsewhere, and she made it clear that she would rather not waste her time by visiting a community that did not have what she was looking for.

In Blake's mind, two issues were at play. First, this lady was very specific about what she wanted, and he did not want to disappoint. Second, the prospect's tone and bluntness indicated that perhaps she had a less-than-stellar opinion of salespeople in general.

Enter video messaging. Blake took his smartphone and walked over to the homesite that he believed would be most appropriate for this prospect. He stood in front of the site and filmed a one-minute video, introducing himself and panning across the property to show the trees.

I'll be honest; the video quality wasn't great. It was bumpy, the audio was inconsistent, and there was nothing polished about it. But that made it awesome! The video was real and raw and personalized. It showed commitment to ease the customer's concerns, and it demonstrated to the prospect that Blake was the kind of sales professional who would go the extra mile.

One other thing to keep in mind: This is a kind of follow-up *in advance*. The prospect had visited the website, so she was very well versed in the offerings of this community. They had spoken by phone, but the customer still had misgivings. Blake could show via video that he was actually a really good guy. That video message caused the customer to show up for the appointment with her guard brought way down.

(On a side note, today websites really do serve as an initial sales presentation. This is the first stop for most customers. With that in mind, a pre-live presentation video really does count as effective follow-up!)

THE VIDEO GENERATION

Today's typical buyer was raised with video as a daily reality: video texts, Snapchat, and other social media sources. According to YouTube, people watched 1 billion hours of video on that platform in 2019. Every. Single. Day.

What was once considered a massive and expensive undertaking (film-ing and editing a video) can now be done with very little effort. The year before smartphones hit the market it would have cost you thousands of dol-lars and hours of time to create what can be done today in minutes and at zero cost.

What's more, your younger prospects *expect* video. They know first-hand that the process of creating video is just not that difficult.

FROM THE FIELD

"I called a couple about a spec home that recently came available. It worked perfect for their time frame. I remembered how they love to walk and really loved the walking trail we had. I sent them a video of me walking on the trail and the new opportunity that came available. They called me back and we met the next day. We spent half of the meeting walking the trail talking about next steps, then we saw the home. They bought the next day. I still see them walk-ing in the community daily."

THE NUMBERS DON'T LIE

Don't take my word for it. These statistics tell the story about the power of video:

- Adding video to an email can increase the open-to-reply rates by up to eight times.[1]

- Prospects who view videos of a product are 85 percent more likely to buy.[2]

- 75 percent of late-stage prospects that received a personalized video closed.[3]

- 87 percent of businesses now use video as a marketing tool.[4]

No doubt about it, video works, and it works well!

One other factoid that is particularly telling: 90 percent of consumers watch video on their mobile devices.[5] Take advantage of that.

WHY SO POWERFUL?

To appreciate the impact of video follow-up you must first understand how the brain processes information. According to the *American Journal of Ophthalmology*, 50 percent of our neural tissue is directly or indirectly related to vision, which assists in visual learning. When our eyes are open, our vision accounts for two-thirds of the electrical activity of the brain. We are, in short, a visual species.

Video is interesting, humanizing, and memorable. Why is it so powerful? Because it engages our emotions.

> *A picture is worth a thousand words . . .*
> *and a video is worth a million pictures.*
> —ANKALA SUBBARAO

We tend to process text in the logical/analytical portion of our brain, while we process video in the emotional core of our brain. You tell me which is more powerful when making a purchase decision.

There is a reason that marketers don't run television ads that do nothing but show the specs and features of a product. No, the commercials instead show what we really want to buy: a better and happier life. That is the power of video.

THE MENTAL POST-IT® NOTE

It's not just what we see that counts; it's what we retain. John Medina, PhD, author of *Brain Rules*, states, "When you pair images with information, people retain 65% of the information three days later, as opposed to just 10% with text alone."

It's more than a marketing message; think of video as something of a Post-it Note for experiences. We attach the video to a specific emotion, and we then find it far easier to retrieve that image down the road.

Suppose you are selling exercise equipment. You can mail a brochure or you can email a series of photos; either would be helpful for your prospects to get a sense of what they can buy. But a video captures something that is far more difficult to see in the photos; it captures emotion. It's not just a matter of seeing how the equipment works; it's about seeing the positive emotional experience of the user.

Want an example? Check out the infomercials for any of the exercise programs put out by Beachbody (P90X, Insanity, T25, CIZE, etc.). What do you see? You see happy people feeling great about their experience. You see the dour "before" image and the celebratory "after" image. It is all intended to engage your emotions and get you to *feel* how good your life can be.

SO WHY DON'T WE SEE MORE OF IT?

We surveyed hundreds of salespeople to gather research for this book and asked, "What percentage of your follow-up is done by various methods (phone, email, face-to-face, text, video, social media)?" Video was only 5 percent!

To be clear, video marketing is booming. But we're not talking about marketing here; we are talking about follow-up. By that I mean personalized and targeted messages that are recorded for specific clients.

Why have so many salespeople failed to catch on to this powerful medium? The answer in one word: discomfort.

It's the discomfort of looking foolish. Or of not knowing how the technical aspects work. Or of just stepping outside of what we normally do. In each case, our desire for comfort constricts our ability to make an impact.

In reality, making a custom video for your prospect is super easy! Once you get the hang of it, you'll want to send videos all day long.

The fact is that video should not be cutting edge, but at the time of this writing it still is. Why? Simply because it is not being used.

STAND OUT!

What a great chance to stand out from the crowd. Do something that offers high impact at zero cost, which *no one else is doing*.

The window is open to maximize the opportunity, but it won't be open for long.

GETTING STARTED

Start small, but start today. I recommend sending a video message to yourself just to get comfortable with the process. For most people, your smartphone has all the equipment you need—no fancy software or SaaS subscription required!

Simply point the camera at a pen or a coffee cup and say a few words. Then text that video to yourself. (If you're stumped on the technical side, just hop over to YouTube and type, "How to send a video text message." You'll find scores of instructional videos that will show you the step-by-step process using any smartphone.) Send several messages to yourself.

Once you are comfortable with the how-to, kick it up a notch and send a message to a friend or family member. Just a quick "thinking about you" message is all it takes. You are simply trying to get used to the process.

Then pick a favorite client, someone you could not possibly offend, and send a quick message. Thank them for their business and let them know you are there to serve at any time.

The point is to start small and safe, and then work your way up to being a video ninja.

CONTENT RULES

Keep in mind: *Content* quality is what counts, not *production* quality. People will give you a lot of leeway if your camera is a bit jumpy or if part of your face is not on the screen. In fact, such amateur-looking videos actually serve to add credibility over the slickly polished commercials we are used to (and bored with).

Don't get hung up on trying to create perfect production quality. The impact is in the effort more than the finished result. In my experience, many salespeople are so afraid of looking silly that they simply give up. Don't do that!

VIDEO: EASY LEVEL

The simplest way to create a video is to point your camera at the product (or some feature of the product that is especially valuable or important to the customer) and do a little narration. You don't need to be on camera; you just need to make sure you are energetic and enthusiastic.

The good news is that this is still a high-impact use of video! And if you are uncomfortable, don't worry; you can re-record over and over until you are satisfied with the result.

VIDEO: ADVANCED LEVEL

You will continue the relational momentum with your client if you include your own smiling face in the video. I know what you're thinking: "I don't like the way I look on camera!" Um . . . I hate to break it to you, but . . . *that is the way you look!*

Your customers already know what you look like. It's *you* who has a problem with your face on video, not the customers. They have already seen you and—this is critical—*they already like you!*

It's not just about sending information. It's also about extending the conversation and sustaining the human relationship. Be bold!

VIDEO: NINJA LEVEL

If you really want to stand out, consider using video to create a future life picture for your customers. The best use of video is when it is customized to the particularities of a specific prospect. Once you get comfortable with this method, you'll find it easy to excel. An extra benefit—it's super fun!

Examples:

- You are selling jewelry, and you just sold an engagement ring. Film a message at a setting that is popular for engagement photos. Super Ninja challenge: Start with a close-up on a sparkly ring and pan out to show the happy bride-to-be hamming unashamedly.

- You are selling cars, and you learn that your potential buyer is into golf. Film yourself standing in front of an open trunk, loading and unloading a golf bag. Super Ninja challenge: Pull out a trophy. A bit of tasteful humor is especially memorable.

- You are selling homes, and your prospect has two dogs. Film a message at a dog park. Super Ninja challenge: Walk a dog in front of one of your home sites and get it to bark enthusiastically on cue.

- You are selling manufacturing equipment. Put an avatar—think of Elf on the Shelf or the Traveling Gnome or Flat Stanley—in or on pieces of equipment: a conveyor, a kettle, an oven, an engine. Super Ninja challenge: Give your avatar a voice with a couple seconds of humorous selling.

Make no mistake—the best videos are personalized videos. Use your imagination!

TIPS FOR GREAT VIDEO CONTENT

1. Keep it short. Consider that the majority of your prospects will view the video on their smartphone. Think 30 seconds max. Fifteen is better.

2. Pick the right setting. Use a pleasant backdrop. Standing with your back to a window will wash out your picture. Standing against a blank wall makes you look like a hostage. Find something visually interesting for the background.

3. If you have any audio, make sure it is clearly understandable.

4. Show high energy. It doesn't have to be over the top, but you must demonstrate a positive emotional experience. Ask yourself: What energy level do I want my customer to adopt? Then be that person.

5. Find the emotion. We are emotional creatures, and we make emotional decisions. Find the emotion in the moment and include that in the video. Happy previous customers make for great salespeople when seen on video!

6. If it's a longer and more involved video, do like the pros and create a *short* storyboard (think of the setting, acceptable light and noise, props, your message). A few minutes of planning helps make sure the pieces come together well without multiple reshoots.

7. Include a call to action. It might be an appointment reminder, a notice that you will call soon, or some other next step. Just think about how you can remind your prospect that the conversation is not over!

> *Good enough is good enough.*
>
> —ANONYMOUS

SENDING VIDEO

One downside to video: It is a red flag for company IT departments. Video files are substantially larger than photos or documents, and many email servers have limits on acceptable file size transfers.

Sending via text message circumvents this issue. As does using a third-party video service such as bombbomb.com.

THE BOTTOM LINE ON VIDEO

I'm all for standing out. I'm all for catching people's valuable attention by doing something unique and memorable. Video elicits emotion, and emotion is memorable. Don't let your fears stand in the way of your success. Be bold. Be unique. Be memorable. Be the difference-maker!

Self-Study Questions:

1. How will you use facial expressions and body language to enhance your message in a video follow-up?

2. What feedback—good and bad—did you get from the test videos you sent to your friends, family, and favorite client? How will you use that to improve?

3. Pick five customers and create short storyboards for follow-up videos for them.

4. How might your videos differ depending on the customer (e.g., millennials vs. seniors)?

Now Do This:

Put this into action right away. Start small if you have to, following the progression laid out in this chapter. Send one to yourself, and then to a friend, and then to a prospect.

Pick one of those customers for whom you've storyboarded and roll camera. Action!

14

Unique Follow-Up Methods

Time to get creative. Time to stand apart.
You cannot copy everyone else's efforts
and think you will get different results.

CREATIVITY HELPS

You can think of follow-up as a tedious and unwanted chore. Or you can approach it as an opportunity for creativity, uniqueness, and yes—fun. Your mental approach is half the battle.

As you read through this important chapter, let me encourage you to really flex your imagination muscles. Don't just get outside the box; get a mile away from the box.

In fact, let me challenge you with this question: What have I missed? Come up with follow-up methods that are unique, unconventional, and memorable.

THE BENEFIT OF UNIQUENESS

We live in a world of sameness. We are marketing copycats. If I dropped you into a major department store chain, you probably couldn't tell me which one you were in unless you saw a sign.

We wear the same jeans. We eat the same french fries. We watch the same teams. Until we don't. Because when someone comes along with a new and different approach, we pay attention.

- Remember when the iPhone first came out? Whether you bought one or not, you knew all about it.
- Coffee used to be boring . . . until Starbucks came along and made it hip.
- Taxi rides were crapshoots at best. Uber changed that game.

In these cases, and so many more, it was the uniqueness that drew our attention. So what about your current follow-up efforts? Can you truly call them unique? If not, why would they stand apart from the noise of all the other marketing that inundates your customer's brain?

> *We don't get a chance to do that many things, and every one should be really excellent. Because this is our life.*
>
> —STEVE JOBS

OPPORTUNITIES

I've listed a number of follow-up opportunities that are, in my opinion, underutilized. Some of them will be newer to you; others will be "old school" techniques.

Look at this list actively. Think about a current prospect, someone who is due for a follow-up outreach. What could you put into action from this list of techniques? Nodding your head and saying, "Yeah, that's a decent idea," will get you nowhere. It is action alone that makes us great.

Here we go . . .

Handwritten Notes

Really, Jeff? You're going to start there? It's like the oldest follow-up method known to man.

That's true; handwritten notes are as old as our ability to write. In fact, for the longest time handwritten notes were the *only* way to follow up.

But let me ask you two questions. First, when was the last time you received a personalized, handwritten note in the mail? Second, if you did receive something personalized and handwritten, did you not move that piece of correspondence to the top of the stack?

The fact is that we rarely receive handwritten notes in society today. But when we do, we esteem them highly. Handwritten notes say, "I cared enough to take the time." If you want an easy way to prove your dedication, here it is.

Five minutes of your time, 50 cents in postage, and bang—you've made an impression.

FROM THE FIELD

"I write a handwritten thank-you note to their address in addition to emails, text, and/or phone calls. I also add two of my business cards in the envelope and say, please give one to your friends or family. Yes, it takes longer, but usually it's a super surprise to them, no matter their age. And the competition has heard about my handwritten notes."

Messenger or Singing Telegram

These are not new, by any means, but they aren't used often anymore. That's the point. Do something unexpected even if it's old-fashioned or out of favor. Would you pay attention if someone came to your door wearing a costume and singing a follow-up message, or would you slam the door in their face? I rest my case.

Social Media

Much has been written about the use of social media for marketing purposes, but what about for follow-up?

It's worth having a presence on social media and putting valuable content there regularly so your customers who are social users will be reminded in a positive way of your existence, but don't expect to use it for follow-up. There is only so much impact you can make on Twitter, Facebook, or Instagram.

The danger: These tools are primarily seen as *social* tools, not business tools. Marketers can certainly attract attention through general targeting, but accomplishing personalized follow-up is quite difficult.

There is, however, a great benefit to social media as an educational tool *for you*. This is a great way to get to know your prospects on a deeper level, and that enhanced knowledge gives you new insights into how to personalize your follow-up. (Don't worry about ethical violations here; if they didn't want the information to be public, they would not have posted it on the Internet in the first place. Just don't overwhelm them with your knowledge of their personal details; you'll look stalkerish.)

Introductions

Suppose you are selling pool installations, a high-priced discretionary purchase. Question: Do you know a good landscaper? Because your client is going to need one.

Consider the product you are selling and ask yourself what else clients might need once they purchase. It might not be something you can provide, but they will definitely appreciate a referral to someone you trust.

Gifts and Swag

Many companies have merchandise lying around the office that would be coveted by a prospect. Is there something you could offer that would be appreciated?

I purchased a hockey stick recently, and the company shipped it to me along with a T-shirt with the company name and logo. It was a $300 hockey stick, and they threw in a $10 T-shirt . . . which I proceeded to wear to the hockey rink around my teammates. That's great marketing!

But there is a deeper reason why this is effective; it goes by the principle of reciprocity. According to Dr. Robert Cialdini in his book *Influence: The Psychology of Persuasion*, people are 13 times more likely to do something for you if you do something for them first.

Want them to return your call? Or to commit to another visit? Send them a gift before you make the ask.

Tickets

I worked in an office environment for years, and there were always free tickets floating around. Minor league baseball games, art and wine festivals, local concerts, movies—all provide excellent opportunities for follow-up (assuming that the size of such a gift does not violate your, or your prospect's, corporate ethics policies).

Remember what we said about the principle of reciprocity. When we do something for others, they notice, they appreciate it, and they will naturally want to repay the gesture in some way. If nothing else, it prevents them from being rude the next time you reach out!

Personalized Video Testimonials from Past Clients

I addressed the use of video in the last chapter, but this is slightly different. People naturally trust those with whom they have something in common.

So find a past client who is in a similar situation as a prospect and interview her for three minutes about her buying experience.

Suppose you are selling vacation properties in a resort area. You are working with a prospect who is interested, but is tentative about tying up such a large sum of money. Call up a past client and head on over with your smartphone. Set up the phone on a tripod and spend three minutes asking questions about his experience. Here's the kicker: Show that customer fully enjoying his new home. Sitting on a deck by a lake, or standing at the first tee, or having a cup of coffee looking out at the skiers.

Your videos don't have to be of you. They may be far more powerful if they feature those who have already made the commitment.

FROM THE FIELD

"I come in early to take pictures or shoot little video clips, then I block time twice a day specifically for follow-up. I force myself to use that time to send relevant information. (It could be something totally unrelated to their search, such as the weather report for Saturday when their child has a ballgame and I'm wishing them good luck. This shows I care and I listened.) This will keep me top of mind. I've found those personal touches are what has propelled my success."

Note from Your Boss or Company Owner

Do you think your boss would take five minutes to write a handwritten note (or even an email) if it meant closing a sale? I think the answer is yes.

Customers absolutely love hearing from the big boss. It makes them feel valued and important. The psychology of honor is an incredibly powerful motivating factor.

Here's the good news: You can write the letter! Just ask your boss to copy and paste the content into an email. Low effort and high payoff. Sounds like a winning formula.

Team Message to a Prospect

I was working with a group of real estate professionals in Atlanta, and I had recommended that each sales professional send a video message to an active prospect. I had one salesperson who took it to the next level; she recruited several of her peers to join in. The salesperson did the talking while her peers stood in the background.

It went something like this: "Carla, you know I want you to be living in this community. I've already told you this is right for you. I want to help you make your dream come true. But I'm not the only one. All my team-mates want you here as well. Right, ladies?"

At that point a group cheer went up from the posse. Put yourself in that prospect's shoes. What is the message? That we out-care the competition!

FROM THE FIELD

"I have coloring books in the office to keep kids busy. I text the photo of what their kids colored and thank them for introducing me to their family."

Note to the Kids or to the Dog

I'm a parent of three and a dog lover. Take care of my kids (including the four-legged kind), and you take care of me.

A note or video to the extended family conveys the idea that you care about the *entire* family. What a kick it would be for the seven-year-old to get a personalized message! And which of your competitors will even think of that idea? (Answer: none!)

Show Your Support

Your prospect competes in triathlons. Or sells his craft beer at street festivals. Or plays softball on Thursday nights.

Why not pay a visit? And while you're there waiting for her to cross the finish line, record that moment and send the video to her afterward.

The point is to see more in your prospect than just dollar signs. Take an interest in the lives of your clients. Get to know them and start to appreciate what makes them unique.

> *Beware of monotony; it's the mother of all deadly sins.*
>
> —EDITH WHARTON

HOW WILL YOU STAND OUT?

Let me conclude with a challenge to be truly unique. I'm not talking about a unique follow-up method; I'm talking about the unique *you*! Great follow-up comes from flexing your creativity muscle and demonstrating your passion. Your customers need exactly that from you. They want you to be creative. They want you to out-care everyone else. They want to have fun during this process.

What do you think? Do you have it in you? Are you up for the challenge to be truly unique?

Self-Study Questions:

1. What is the most creative follow-up you've ever received from a sales rep . . . or anyone else? How could you adapt the approach to use with your own customers?

2. It's easy to get stuck in a rut. When have you been most proud of your creative follow-up? How can you get those creative juices flowing again?

3. Take off your selling hat so your brain has room to expand. Now jot down 10 of the craziest ideas you can think of for creative follow-up. Now put your hat back on and tweak two of them for practical application.

4. Spend a few minutes brainstorming with your colleagues or with your family about creative follow-up. Capture *all* the ideas. Which of these ideas can you apply now in following up with your customers?

5. Would your teammates or your boss be willing to participate in your follow-up actions? If you don't know, ask them.

Now Do This:

Think of a prospect you have been working with, someone with whom you have a good relationship. Now look through the ideas in this chapter and select just one that you can do right away.

Did you do it? Was it fun? I think you probably just nodded yes. Great! Now do it again!

15

Follow-Up Scripts

With the strategy and structure of the call now in place, it is helpful to have some "jump starts" to help plan for the most effective conversations.

TO SCRIPT OR NOT TO SCRIPT

Should you script out your messages so that you can gain the efficiency of a "write it once, do it a thousand times" strategy?

On the one hand, there is a compelling argument for crafting your follow-up message one time perfectly and then simply cutting and pasting thereafter. You don't want to have to strain your brain for just the right words for every email interaction. I like the idea of starting with the perfect phrasing and then adjusting it as you go along.

On the other hand, scripts sound like . . . well . . . scripts. We all know when someone is reading to us, or when we receive a form email that has likely gone out to dozens, hundreds, or even thousands of others. It just doesn't sound authentic.

Great actors are great for a reason: They can take someone else's words and meanings and make them their own. That's not easy to do.

SCRIPTS VERSUS SPEAKING POINTS

A better way to approach this would be to adjust your nomenclature. Instead of scripts, consider preparing speaking bullet points. Scripts imply rigidness and inflexibility. Speaking points are malleable and easily adapted to meet the need.

When I am delivering a webinar or when I'm recording one of my Five-Minute Sales Training videos for my YouTube channel (search "Jeff Shore Sales Training" on YouTube), I have a series of speaking points in front of me. Frankly, a script would totally throw me off and would prevent me from delivering in a natural tone. I would be thinking so much about getting the words right that I would probably sound robotic.

> *The fun stuff comes when someone is not so strict on sticking to the script. You're allowed the spontaneity, and great moments can happen.*
>
> —JENNIFER ANISTON

Let me offer you a series of speaking points to meet the various follow-up methods. These are just my suggestions. I *strongly* recommend that you rewrite them in your own voice. Keep them at the ready for easy reference during your Lead Conversion Hour. (That, my friends, is a tease. We'll dive deep into the Lead Conversion Hour in the next chapter.)

FOR PHONE CALLS

Remember that your tone is more important than your words. So before you think about word choices, focus first on the energy that you wish to express. Your customer will pick up on your Emotional Altitude long before they process your actual message. (Remember to smile into the phone!)

When drafting your speaking points:

- Think strategy first, specifics second. What are you trying to accomplish? What is your overall goal? If you cannot answer those questions, don't call!

- Draft in bullet points; speak in sentences. No one wants to be read to. They want to believe they are having an organic conversation with a real human being.

- Practice first. Practice your "phone voice" with someone on your team. Ask them if your conversation sounds scripted or choppy.

- Make it your own. You must sound like *you*, not some telemarketer version of you.

THE INTRODUCTION

The first few seconds of a follow-up phone call are the most critical. Your energy and tone will speak volumes. Set the scene for a helpful conversation.

DON'T SAY:	DO SAY:
"Hi, it's Phil from ABC Services. How are you?"	*"Hi, it's Phil from ABC Services, calling you as I promised. How is your day going?"*
Very awkward for a customer. There is no relational connection.	This is far more conversational, and it ties back to the last interaction.
"Is this a good time for a chat?"	*"I have the information you requested. Do you have two minutes for me to share that with you?"*
How long is a "chat"? This is too vague, and it leaves the door open for an unfavorable response.	Two minutes is a reasonable request and is nonthreatening to a customer.

THE VALUE-ADD

Too many follow-up calls are about the salesperson's agenda. You must quickly establish the fact that you are there to serve and to add value.

DON'T SAY:	DO SAY:
"Just following up to see if you received the information I sent you."	*"I hope the information I sent you last week was helpful. I've got one more idea that I think will help even more. May I tell you what I'm thinking?"*
There is no real value being offered in that statement. It's a call you are making for you, not for them.	Now it's not just value; it's added value. It lets the prospect know that you are constantly looking for solutions.
"I haven't heard back from you. Wanted to know if you were still interested."	*"I know you're super busy, but I've got something you'll want to hear. Do you have two minutes?"*
Let me count the number of times that approach has actually worked with a prospect. Zero.	Even for the "super busy," two minutes is a reasonable request if you can make life easier in some way.

FROM THE FIELD

"I try to always follow up with a unique value proposition just for them."

THE CALL TO ACTION

Never begin a follow-up call unless you have an end point in mind. Determine the next steps and turn it into a call to action.

DON'T SAY:	*DO SAY:*
"I'd like to talk further, so we can move this along and get you started using our services. When is a good time for you?"	*"I've taken some time to customize a few solutions for you, and I'd like to sit down for fifteen minutes and show you what I've done. Can we meet on Friday?"*
Note that there is no value add, no reason to sit down, nothing specific in the offering, and the pressure is on the client to pick a good time. That's a losing proposition from front to back.	It's a simple request, it's a limited amount of time on a designated day, and you have already taken the time to prepare something. Very difficult to say no.

Remember these points from Chapter 10 when making follow-up phone calls:

- Refresh the relationship in your mind. Pick a personal connection point.
- Get to the purpose of your call as soon as possible.
- Provide a service (give).
- Ask a temperature close question.
- Get to your objective (close, second appointment, etc.).
- Agree on the next step.
- End on a positive and happy note.

FOR VOICE MAIL

Voice-to-voice is hands-down the most effective manner of communication. But if your customer does not pick up, you can still communicate an enticing and exciting message. You don't need to be over-the-top giddy, but you need to convey excitement and energy in your tone.

Of course, you would prefer to have a voice-to-voice conversation, so I offer this rule-of-thumb: Don't leave a voice mail until your third attempt at a voice-to-voice call. The voice mail requires that the prospect takes further action (returns the call), and that puts you out of control. That said, after a couple of calls with no message, it becomes obnoxious to the prospect. At that point, leave a message.

The overriding key to effectiveness in voice mail: let people know that you have something they want.

DON'T SAY:	DO SAY:
"Hi, it's Phil from ABC Services. I'd like to talk to you as soon as I can. Can you call me back at 555-555-5555?"	*"Hi, it's Phil from ABC Services. Sorry I missed you, but I've been doing some research on your situation and I want to share what I have found. I think it will help you in your planning process. Can we plan on a five-minute phone call sometime this afternoon?"*
Uh . . . why? What reason does the prospect have for calling you back? There is nothing to be gained here.	Can you sense the intrigue? There is something that has been done specifically for the prospect that will make his or her life easier. That's worth five minutes.

FOR EMAIL

As I mentioned in Chapter 9, email is not the preferred method of follow-up unless you are using it for data, attachments, photos, and so on.

If you are going to send an email, pay very close attention to both the subject line and the first line of the message. Like a phone call, you must communicate value being shared, but you must make that clear very, very quickly. If you cannot grab the recipient right away, your message is destined to end up in the virtual trash.

DON'T SAY:	*DO SAY:*
"Thank you for your interest in Acme Ventures line of products."	*"Shelly, I know you are frustrated with _____, and I'm sending you something that I think will help."*
Can you feel the impersonal nature of that opening line? That's a deleted message waiting to happen.	Clearly personal, clearly caring, and clearly applicable.
"We have the _____ of your dreams, and we are just waiting for you to take advantage of an exciting new offer."	*"John, we are just starting to roll out a new program that I think you'll want to take a look at. It addresses your need for _____."*
Thank you, marketing guru, for that well-written piece of junk mail.	Again, the applicability to the customer's situation is what matters most.

Here's an idea: Go back and look at the last 20 follow-up emails you have sent. Evaluate them according to the guidelines I have laid out. Did they pass the test? Did they get results?

FOR TEXT

Like a phone call or an email, every text message should have a clear purpose. The strategy must precede the execution. So before you send a text message, ask yourself: What's the point? What am I trying to convey and accomplish?

Acceptable purposes include:

- Checking your prospect's availability for a call or meeting
- Confirming a call or meeting
- Sending a helpful resource link
- Briefly (very briefly) answering a question the prospect asked earlier

Unacceptable reasons include:

- Just "checking in"
- Asking why the prospect didn't return your call or email
- Reiterating your product's features or benefits without adding value
- Sending anything that exceeds two paragraphs

DON'T SAY:	DO SAY:

> "Hey, dude. Haven't heard from you in a while. What's up?"

Very appropriate for your best man; entirely inappropriate in a business setting.

> "Hi, it's Phil. Just confirming our four o'clock appointment. Talk to you then."

Short, sweet, and helpful.

> "I wanted to tell you about an exciting change to the Vintage Gold plan we were talking about earlier. It can save you a ton of money and make a big difference in your day-to-day life. And the program comes with an extended warranty backed by 45 years of dedicated service and consistently high customer satisfaction marks. Not that it matters; you stopped reading this text about 40 words ago, so now I'm going to ramble on about absolutely nothing of importance . . ."

C'mon, man! Just stop. Nobody wants to read a text this long.

> "Hi, it's Phil. Do yourself a favor and check out the Buyer's Mind podcast on iTunes. It's definitely up your alley."

Add value wherever and whenever you can.

WHATEVER YOU DO . . . BE YOURSELF!

Part of the reason I use speaking points instead of a script is that I want to encourage real interaction, leaving the door open for creativity and synergy with my customer, which makes for an authentic conversation. It also keeps things fresh for me, helping me to stay alert and enthusiastic. Imagine reading the same-old, same-old script every time you make a follow-up call. It would scare off all but the politest customers, and it would bore you to tears!

> *You start on a voyage; you know where you will end up but not what will occur along the way. You want to be surprised.*
>
> —FEDERICO FELLINI

How can you start sounding less like a robot and more like an authentic, interested, and positive-energy human being who is looking out for the customer?

Self-Study Questions:

1. What do you hate about scripted follow-up that you receive? Why is it annoying?

2. How do you keep yourself fresh during your follow-up time? What do you do to ensure you are not sounding like a script?

3. Next time you get a robocall, listen to the script. What tips you off that it's a spammy message and not something of value? Do you have any of those elements in your own follow-up scripts?

4. Record a few voice messages you leave for customers. (Note: Don't record live conversations without getting permission!) How well did you deliver enticing and exciting messages?

5. Check your last five follow-up texts. How do they match the "do say" and "don't say" guidelines?

Now Do This:

Select three customers who may be ready for a follow-up outreach. Create bulleted speaking points. Get yourself psyched, and make the call! The idea is to train yourself on how to make your follow-up natural and effective.

16

The Perfect Lead Conversion Hour

Effective follow-up is about establishing the habits of lead conversion success. It's about rituals and routines, rhythms and the right attitude. It's about not quitting when others give up. It's about the extra effort that separates you from everyone else.

EVERYDAY RITUALS

What are the important rituals in your life? I'm going to go out on a limb and suggest that brushing your teeth is a vital twice-a-day (or more) ritual that you simply do not miss, as would be your morning coffee and checking Facebook or Instagram. Prayer would also qualify for many of you.

These are all examples of rituals that no one forces us to do. We do these either because:

- We enjoy them
- We know that they are good for us

Ultimately, the most effective rituals are those that check both of those boxes.

SUCCESS RITUALS

Let's get more specific. What about success rituals? What are the rituals that make athletes victorious? Or artists? Or students? What are those particular daily habits that introduce success over a period of time?

When you think about it, success in all areas of life comes about when we do the important things that others are not willing to do. Top musicians put in more rehearsal time. Athletes practice the same plays over and over.

Writing a book is a difficult endeavor. It is the kind of task, like follow-up, that is easily prioritized as "when I get around to it." Like so many authors, I can only complete a book when I dedicate specific times to the effort when my schedule is open and my mind is fresh. For me, writing is a ritual.

For top-performing sales professionals, follow-up is not a task; it is a ritual. It is a daily habit.

I want to encourage you to think differently about your approach to follow-up. Stop thinking in terms of duty, responsibility, burden, or task. Start thinking in terms of opportunity, victory, success, and even enjoyment.

THE LEAD CONVERSION HOUR

Stop reading for a moment, set the book aside, and open your calendar app. Look at your schedule for tomorrow and find an open hour (preferably early in the day). Enter a one-hour appointment for yourself and label it the Lead Conversion Hour.

This 60-minute block of time can change your career and your life. One hour, early in the day, of complete and total focus on follow-up.

> *Until we can manage time, we can manage nothing else.*
>
> —Peter Drucker

Think about the benefits of a full hour of follow-up time first thing in the morning:

- You are fresh; your mental energy is strong. This happens before the trials of the day sap your mental strength.

- You are calling prospects while they are mentally fresh. Like you, they get weary as the day goes on. Wouldn't you prefer to have a conversation while the energy is higher?*

- You've given the rest of the day for prospects to return calls if you did not catch them initially. Makes sense, right? If you call them at 4:30 p.m., by the time they return your call you're at home watching *Shark Tank*.

- You gain energy for the rest of the day. You know how you feel when you get your workout done first thing in the morning? It's a victory that lasts the remainder of the day. That's how it is with follow-up that is done first thing in the morning.

- You gain momentum. It's not like you finish the Lead Conversion Hour and then take a nap. By that point you are feeling strong and accomplished, ready to take on the world.

- You get sales! That's right; in one hour's time you are moving the ball down the field for a strong number of prospects. You are doing what your competitors are not, and you are gaining the victories that they can only dream about.

> *The key is not to prioritize what's on your schedule, but to schedule your priorities.*
> —STEPHEN COVEY

---

* For more on this subject, go to jeffshore.com/podcast and listen to my interview with Dan Pink on his book *When: The Scientific Secrets of Perfect Timing*.

THE LEAD CONVERSION HOUR MINDSET

What do you want to be thinking about in your preparation time?

- Achievement drive: You have to win. You *have* to. It's in your DNA.
- Obsession: This is not a program, and it is not a task. This is something that consumes you.
- Energy: You have so much positive liveliness that your energy is adopted by your prospects.
- Goals: You know precisely what you want to accomplish, and you power forward without resting.
- Uniqueness: You stand out from everyone else because you do what they will not do.

How badly do you want it? How much do you need to be successful? Because the ritual of the Lead Conversion Hour will get you there!

> *Lost time is never found again.*
>
> —Benjamin Franklin

PLANNING THE LEAD CONVERSION HOUR

Proper planning makes for top performance. Just a little bit of preparation time will go a long, long way toward your success. Follow these steps:

Make an Appointment with Yourself

The key is to look at this as a specific, timed appointment. Think of it like you are setting an appointment with the owner of your company. Nothing would get in the way of making that appointment, and nothing would distract you during the appointment.

Manage the Distractions

Managing potential distractions is critical to your success. Get rid of every barrier you can think of. That includes human distractions. Let people know—in no uncertain terms—that this hour is vital to your success and that you cannot be interrupted.* Think like a doctor performing surgery; she would likely not pause the surgery to take a phone call from one of her kids!

One extraordinarily successful sales pro that I trained now puts a sign on his office door during his Lead Conversion Hour: "Lead Conversion Conversations in Progress. Do Not Disturb . . . unless your hair is on fire or a talking dog shows up." It's quite effective.

> *It is not enough to be busy. . . .*
> *The question is: what are we busy about?*
> —HENRY DAVID THOREAU

Rules for the Lead Conversion Hour

1. No distractions. I know I've already said that, but distractions are the number-one killer of effective Lead Conversion time. It bears repeating. Everyone knows not to disturb your Lead Conversion Hour!

2. No more than 30 seconds between each call or contact. The longer you wait to make the next call, the easier it is to lose your

---

* For more on removing distractions, read Cal Newport's groundbreaking book *Deep Work*. It will change your life!

momentum. You should pause only long enough to review the purpose of your next call.

3. Embrace discomfort. There will be calls that you do not want to make. Make them anyway. Your brain will be happy to offer justifying stories as to why you should *not* make the call. Tell that part of your brain to shut up and go away. Just keep pounding the phone!

Prepare a Call List in Advance

The goal during the Lead Conversion Hour is to make as many quality contacts as you can. Do the prep work on deciding whom to call and why to call before the hour begins. That will prevent you from becoming bogged down during the call time.

USING YOUR CRM

Your lead-tracking software can be your secret weapon . . . or your brutish taskmaster. As a general observation, those sales professionals who are most diligent in their follow-up efforts are also those who know how to leverage their CRM as a significant strategic advantage. The converse is also true; those who shun their CRM tend to be those who likewise avoid follow-up activities.

What is it to you: a tool or a tyrant? Your perspective will go a long way toward your success . . . or lack thereof. You can make that decision right this moment.

Having made that decision to embrace the CRM (that is your decision, yes?), you now must decide how to use it effectively. The fact is that most CRM systems are completely overloaded with features. This can be a real problem because often salespeople are overwhelmed by all the bells and whistles.

In this case, take a lesson from pilots. A commercial jetliner has hundreds of dials and gauges, but only six are really worth paying attention to:

- Airspeed indicator
- Altimeter
- Vertical speed indicator
- Attitude indicator
- Heading indicator
- Turn coordinator

Wow! Some of these are good descriptors of what you might be gauging during a follow-up call. Are you going at the right speed? Do you have the right (emotional) altitude? Do you need to adjust the way the discussion is heading? If yes, how do you coordinate a turn in the conversation?

The simplicity of the six-dial air navigation approach is a good metaphor for your CRM. There are a ton of features that can be utilized; you need to determine which few will meet your needs the best. I recommend finding that salesperson on your team who is most proficient at follow-up and asking for his or her input on how to optimize the CRM. It is far more impactful to use four features really well than to use 40 features haphazardly.

THE PERFECT HOUR

> *It is well to be up before daybreak, for such habits contribute to health, wealth, and wisdom.*
>
> —ARISTOTLE

I'm not asking for a predawn commitment. After all, most of your customers won't even be awake then. But let your imagination run wild for a moment . . .

It's 8:55 a.m. You've had your coffee, you've said hello to your work-mates, you've addressed any burning issues of the morning. You had some excellent focus time where you got into a positive frame of mind and pre-pared for a successful day. You are mentally fresh and ready to change the lives of your customers.

You sit down and block out all distractions. No Twitter. No music. No interruptions. It's just you and your leads. Your opportunities are on the screen in front of you, and you are excited to jump in.

The clock hits 9:00 a.m. and the power hour begins. You are dialing with a smile on your face, the first of many calls that you will make within the hour. You reach someone's voice mail, leave an encouraging message, and immediately make your next call.

Over the course of the hour you make 15 calls, write 11 emails, fire off eight text messages, and record three video messages. You have spo-ken directly with five prospects and secured follow-up appointments with three of them.

It's still only 10 a.m., and the rest of the day lies in front of you. How are you feeling? Successful? Accomplished? Happy? Satisfied?

It's not a pipe dream, my friends. You can have that feeling of success every single day.

FROM THE FIELD

The only inhibitor to follow-up is not time, but rather not schedul-ing specific time for follow-up or lead conversion activities. If it's booked, it happens!

FOLLOW-UP AS A HABIT

> *If you believe you can change—if you make*
> *it a habit—the change becomes real.*
>
> —CHARLES DUHIGG

Think of follow-up not as a chore or a task but as a habit. Like flossing your teeth or putting your phone away during dinner, it's just plain good for you. And like all other habits, it takes a while to develop.

That is why putting your Lead Conversion Hour on your calendar is so very important. You are setting an appointment with yourself and making it a top priority. Trust me. If you do it enough, you won't even think about it.

If you cannot get an entire hour in because of other commitments or problems that arise, then schedule 30 minutes. Or even 10. But do it consistently. You want to be in the rhythm of lead conversion *every single workday.*

FROM THE FIELD

"I start my day 30 minutes before the doors open, and that is when I do my follow-up. I do not check my voice mail or emails when I first walk in; only follow up!"

When you look at the most successful people in life, they can be defined by a commitment to good habits. This is one habit that will pay off for the rest of your career. What is stopping you?

Self-Study Questions:

1. What is keeping you from doing a full hour for lead conversion at the start of the day?

2. Do you say, "I'll just do a quick email/text check" before you start on lead conversions? If so, how long does that take? Go ahead. Measure that "quick check" for five days.

3. If you're a night owl, what are you missing out on by *not* putting a Lead Conversion Hour *early* in the day?

4. Scientists say it takes *a minimum* of 21 days to form a new habit. (More recent studies show 66 days!) Are you ready to stick with doing your Lead Conversion Hour for 66 workdays? Mark each day on your calendar as proof. At the end, voilà, a new habit!

Now Do This:

Open your calendar now and get that Lead Conversion Hour scheduled as a recurring daily entry right away. Let others know that this is a nonnegotiable priority and that there must be no interruptions. Your fervor will go a long way toward managing others, but it will also reinforce your own commitment.

Commit to launching your follow-up efforts to new heights.

17

Waking Up Old Leads

Here you will find a strategy that countless salespeople have found invaluable in their follow-up process. Discipline, simplicity, effectiveness—you get it all in one package.

DON'T GIVE UP

Throughout this book I have shared the opinion that good follow-up is fast follow-up, and that the longer prospects stay in the decision-making process without purchasing, the less likely it is that they will purchase at all. Emotion tends to wane with every passing day and, since we make purchase decisions based primarily on our emotional needs, the buying impulse diminishes.

That said, there are most certainly occasions where circumstances bring the buying consideration to a premature halt and prospects walk away for a period of time. Which raises the question: How do you reengage prospects after some amount of time has passed?

> *I got lucky because I never gave up the search. Are you quitting too soon? Or are you willing to pursue luck with a vengeance?*
>
> —JILL KONRATH

CASE STUDY

Michelle has grown weary of her car. She is driving the practical compact sedan that, when she first bought it, was cute and lovable but is now old and out of style. Her repair bills continue to increase, her windshield has a growing fault line, and she cannot identify the source of an increasingly musty smell emanating from the direction of the glove compartment.

In short, Michelle has an increasing dissatisfaction. She doesn't hate the car and there is no pressing reason why she has to replace it today, but she is on the dissatisfaction downslope.

Michelle is thinking about buying a new car. Not just any car, her dream car—a slick convertible with all the bells and whistles. It is a car she has thought about since the very first time she watched the movie *Pretty Woman*. It is more than a car; it is a statement. And that statement says, "I'm at a point in my life where I can drive whatever I want and for whatever reason I want it, without owing anyone an explanation."

Michelle has an increasing Future Promise in the form of her dream car. Her emotion wells up when she so much as thinks about the new ride.

While her Current Dissatisfaction and Future Promise are both elevated, Michelle is nevertheless afflicted by both Cost and Fear. The price—and corresponding payment—is high, especially given that her current car is fully paid off. She is worried about being financially tied down. What if she buys the car only to find that she doesn't like it as much as she thought she would? And can she trust the salesperson? And . . .

Fast-forward to the point where Michelle is engaged in an ongoing conversation with a sales rep who is eager to get her into that new convertible. The test drive was a success, and the financing plan is in place.

All looks like a go . . . until the roof of Michelle's home springs a massive leak and Michelle is forced into a $20,000 second loan on her home to have the roof replaced. The dream car is now on hold.

RAMIFICATIONS

Consider what Michelle is going through and ask yourself:

- Is Michelle's dissatisfaction with her current car any less than it was?
- Will her dissatisfaction increase over time?
- Does she still love the idea of purchasing her dream convertible?
- Will that Future Promise get stronger in the future?

Bottom line: The factors that put Michelle in the market for a new car are still there. They're just lying dormant while she recovers from the financial blow.

It is my contention that 99.8 percent of all sales reps would call it a day at this point. After all, Michelle cannot buy the car if she doesn't have the money. The financial setback turned her into a nonbuyer.

Or did it?

Remember that the factors that spurred her buying activity are still in place. She still has a problem that needs to be solved.

In other words, it's not a question of if; it is only a question of when.

WHAT ABOUT YOUR PROSPECTS?

Swap out Michelle for the name of a past prospect. Swap out car for whatever it is you sell. Swap out roof for whatever setback took your client off the path.

Now ask: Is your prospect still out there, and does he or she still have a problem that needs to be solved? If the answer is yes, then your job is not done.

Life, as you may have observed, is complicated. At the same time that your prospects are moving through their buying progression, they are dealing with a difficult boss, problem teenagers, health issues, and an assortment of other stresses associated with adulting.

I was shopping for a nice road bike and was very close to making a purchase. On the very morning I was planning to head back to the bike store (for the third time) with the intention of purchasing, I injured my calf muscle in a weird misstep on the staircase. I couldn't even walk, let alone ride a bike. That injury cost me four months of rehab.

The salesperson at the bike shop thought he had a sale. He knew I was very interested, and I'm sure he expected to see me that day. And then I ghosted him. Life got in the way, and he didn't see me for months.

What are you going to do if you are the sales professional? How do you reconnect with a prospect if it's been months since your last conversation?

> *Our greatest weakness lies in giving up. The most certain way to succeed is always to try just one more time.*
>
> —THOMAS EDISON

THE 5 + 5 + 5 FOLLOW-UP SYSTEM

At this very moment you have a long list of stale leads, people with whom you have spoken in the past and whom you once considered viable prospects, but for whom the trail has gone cold for one reason or another. If you are like most salespeople, you find it very awkward to call such a person after a significant time lapse and try to figure out how to reignite the relationship.

You need a system. Something that could work for *all* your leads, but that works especially well for stale leads.

I've got just the ticket. It's called the 5 + 5 + 5 system:

- Five handwritten notes
- Five days
- Five phone calls

Here's how it works.

THE FIRST FIVE: FIVE HANDWRITTEN NOTES

I wrote about the power of the handwritten note in Chapter 14. People pay attention to notes received via snail mail because they are so rare. Take advantage of that.

Find an old lead, check your notes, and then ask these three important questions:

1. Why was this prospect looking in the first place, and what has likely happened since?

2. What has changed in my value proposition that this prospect might find intriguing?

3. How can I reconnect on a personal point?

Now grab a note card and start writing. Short, upbeat, personal, and compelling. The key is the call to action in the note, and it comes in the form of this important sentence:

"I'll call you in a couple of days to discuss further."

That important line sets up the forthcoming phone call.

In our example from the beginning of the chapter, that note might look something like this:

Michelle, I hope you're doing well and that the work project you were managing when we last spoke was a success. We've got some new alternatives on financing here that I believe could lower your car payment even more. It will take me two minutes to explain. I'll call you in a couple of days to discuss further.

—Jeff

That's it. A time investment of a couple of minutes and a cost investment of a stamp and a note card. And you just *dramatically* increased your chances of a healthy restart to the conversation in the near future.

One other thing: Include your business card with the note. If prospects are particularly interested, they will want to call you right away!

Make sense? Great! Now get to work and write a handwritten note to five different prospects today. And tomorrow. And the next day. And . . .

FROM THE FIELD

"I still remember sitting on my bed at home 17 years ago [when I was] just starting in the industry, debating whether I should call a prospective buyer after a couple weeks. I told myself, why not? He became one of my greatest advocates, and I received numerous referrals from him, which really helped launch my career today. Glad I called that guy."

THE SECOND FIVE: FIVE DAYS

It's called snail mail for a reason; it will take a few days for that note to get to your prospect. Don't worry; you won't be bored. Each day you'll be writing five more notes. You are building up a list of people who will be waiting for your call!

Now consider how your note will be received.

First, it will be novel because of the rarity of such correspondence.

Second, it will refresh both your relationship and the recollection of the initial purchase consideration. The prospect will revisit the positive emotional state that she experienced at the time.

Finally, the principle of reciprocity will kick into gear. You did something kind and thoughtful for your prospect; you sent a personal note. It would be very bad form to repay that kindness with rudeness. Is it possible? Of course. But a rude reply would likely be an indication that the relationship was never all that good.

THE THIRD FIVE: FIVE PHONE CALLS

Five days have elapsed since you sent that note; it's time to make the phone call. Let me offer a few tips on how to get the most out of that conversation.

(You might also want to revisit Chapter 10 to refresh your thinking on telephone follow-up.)

- Make that call early in the day as part of your Lead Conversion Hour. You're fresh, your prospect is fresh, and you'll give prospects the entire day to respond if you don't reach them with that initial call.

- Begin by rekindling the relationship. Ask about the job, the kids, the cat, the hobby. Let your prospect know that the initial interaction meant something to you.

- Take the temperature, and make it assumptive. I would not recommend asking, "So, are you still interested in a new car?" That verbiage will put your customer into a defensive posture right from the start. Instead, try something like this: "I'm assuming you are still interested in purchasing a new car, and I wanted to talk about some changes to our financing program that I think will interest you. Can I take two minutes to do that?" That is your moment of truth. If she is no longer a prospect, she'll let you know right away. If she gives you permission to share, it's time to get really excited!

THE 5 + 5 + 5 HABIT

This is not a program that you try for just a couple days. The payoff of this system comes over time. But think about the potential.

Suppose you follow the system just as described for the next three months. That's 13 weeks times 5 days a week times 5 contacts per day. Do the math.

13 weeks
× 5 days
× 5 contacts per day
325 contacts made

Now suppose that you can get just a 5 percent conversion rate from those contacts. That's not a stretch, given that these are all people who have shown an interest in the past. A 5 percent conversion rate will net you *16* additional sales over the course of a quarter. How would you feel about those results?

> *Great things are done by a series of small things brought together.*
>
> —VINCENT VAN GOGH

Keep in mind that you have to be diligent to do this. Don't skip a day. Not following up on old leads is a guaranteed missed shot. Why not go for it?

Self-Study Questions:

1. How do you currently track old high-probability leads? Or do you just forget them?

2. What would 16 more conversions a quarter mean for you? Think about the results and what it could do for your career and your life. Is it worth a few minutes a day?

3. The best thing that could happen from following the 5 + 5 + 5 system is a sales conversion from an old lead, but what is the worst that would happen if the customer isn't interested?

4. If you do not wish to use the 5 + 5 + 5 system, what will you do with your stale leads? What better way is there to rekindle the connection?

Now Do This:

Try it for one quarter, starting today. One full quarter. See if it doesn't make a dramatic impact—on you and on your customer.

18

When to Let Go

Sometimes it's just not going to happen. But before you throw in the towel, are you sure? If you want to sleep well at night, you need the assurance that you took that sale as far as it could go before you called it quits.

HOW FAR SHOULD YOU GO?

What would an old-school sales manager say about follow-up technique? (When I say old-school, I'm referring to that rude, disrespectful, testosterone-driven lunatic sales manager. Think Alec Baldwin in *Glengarry Glen Ross*.) How would he encourage follow-up? In all likelihood the sales meeting would include soundbites like this:

- "If they aren't cussing at you, you haven't gone far enough with your follow-up."
- "I want cease-and-desist letters from attorneys, people. Harass them until they sue us."
- "Hound those prospects until they buy or die. And if they die, go after their kids!"

Sound about right? It's everything we hate about sales.

But it does raise an important question: How far should you go? And how do you know when you are in danger of crossing the line?

Let's start with a reality check. Just how likely is it that customers are going to cuss at you when you are making a follow-up call? And if they do, what commentary did that offer on the value of the relationship in the first place?

I am of the opinion that many salespeople are so afraid of offending a prospect that they pull up *way* short of the necessary effort it will take to secure a sale. That is a flawed mindset right out of the gate because it presupposes that follow-up is not a valuable service but rather an annoying nuisance.

Is it worth occasionally going a bit too far in order to learn the limits? I think that risk might be worth it.

FROM THE FIELD

"Follow-up fails happen daily. You have to remember that this is not something to take personally. For every *no* you receive, you're one step closer to that *yes!*"

There is a hockey drill that I use when I'm at a skating practice. I take a five-gallon bucket and turn it upside down. I put one hand on the bucket and then skate in circles around it, extending my arm and leaning more with every turn, as my feet get farther away in an expanding circle. By the time I am at maximum extension I feel like I am nearly parallel with the ice, with my arm extended far from my body. One fraction of an inch and I will fall.

And that is precisely what I want to do. I want to fall because it is the only way I learn just how far I can lean. Sometimes you have to fail in order to prove to yourself just how far you can push.

THE THREE-QUESTION TEST

I have suggested throughout this book that effective follow-up requires dedication and perseverance. The winners press forward when others give up.

How do you know when you've reached the end of the line? At what point do you throw in the towel? Or is that whole "buy-or-die" thing actually good advice?

I would argue that it is never beneficial to throw solid efforts at non-prospects. There is a time when you should, in fact, say "so long" to your old leads.

Before you do, however, ask a few important questions.

1. "Did My Customer Give Me a Clear and Compelling Reason to Shut Down My Follow-Up Efforts?"

The "buy-or-die" advice would suggest that the wishes of the prospect do not matter. But what if your customer tells you, "We just completed a sale with another company. Thank you for your help, but you don't need to call me again."

Would you call again? I wouldn't. Why? Because I only call prospects, and this person is no longer a prospect. My time is valuable, and I would rather talk to people who might actually buy.

Others might disagree. They might suggest, "That person can still refer someone else to buy." That's true, but isn't it also true for every other non-buyer out there? Is it worth my diligent follow-up in the hope of getting a referral from a nonclient? And if someone was going to refer, I would hope that it was based on the efforts and attention that I had already invested.

Having said that, this is where your automated follow-up comes into play via your CRM platform. You can still set up your former prospect for ongoing communication. I am only suggesting that an ongoing phone follow-up campaign will yield unacceptable results.

2. "Did I Take This Sales Effort as Far as It Would Go?

Is there one more thing I could still do to keep this sale alive?" This is actually an excellent question to ask after every single sales conversation, but particularly effective in evaluating your follow-up efforts. You're considering throwing in the towel on a prospect in whom you've invested a lot of time and energy. It is worth your time to do a gut check first.

Think creatively here. Ask for someone else's opinion. Talk to your sales manager. Was there one more step, one more action, one more thing you could have tried?

Bottom line: Make the prospect absolutely prove that you should move on. You want to be able to rest well, knowing you did everything you could do.

3. "Am I Being Honest with Those Answers, or Did I Just Lie to Myself?"

Enough said, right?

BEWARE THE RATIONALIZATION

Ask any sales manager in any sales industry, and they will tell you about one particular type of sales representative. It's that salesperson who will take all the credit when things go right and place all the blame elsewhere when things go wrong.

In the first quarter, it's, "Man, did I bust my butt to get my numbers. I played every card in the deck, I worked late hours, and I have never been smoother on my closing questions. Despite everything that was working against me, I made my numbers anyway."

In the second quarter, it's, "The leads coming in off the website have dramatically decreased in quality. Meanwhile, my sales manager is nowhere to be found, and I *still* haven't gotten the spec change I requested three months ago. I can't be expected to make my numbers without support."

What I have just shared is an example of what psychologists call "attribution theory." As it applies to this scenario, that salesperson is thinking: "If it went right, it was me; if it went wrong, it was someone or something else."

What does this have to do with follow-up? Plenty. Far too many salespeople make the mistake of giving up too early; I think we can all agree on that. But then they increase the damage done by convincing themselves that quitting was the right thing to do. They even have the stories to prove it.

- "My prospects always buy in the first 60 days. That guy had gone 90 without making a decision. He was never going to buy."
- "I will risk damage to the brand if I keep calling this person."
- "No one likes to be harassed. Doing so would be inconsistent with my reputation for providing stellar customer service."
- "Guys like that buy on price alone, and we are not the lowest price."

Notice the underlying sentiment in all of those stories: *I did my job!*

Bottom line: Are you giving up because it's easy for you or because it is best for your prospects?

> *Most of the important things in the world have been accomplished by people who have kept on trying when there seemed to be no hope at all.*
>
> —DALE CARNEGIE

WHEN YOU RUN OUT OF REASONS

One of the principal reasons that salespeople discontinue their follow-up efforts is that they simply run out of reasons to call. They don't want to call and say, "Hi, just checking in," so they don't call at all.

My advice: Come up with more reasons! Can you be too much help to your prospect? I think not. The Internet alone can provide you with dozens of value-adds that would pave the way for continued follow-up.

And if the Internet doesn't come through for you, ask your peers. Lay out the scenario and ask for help. "What would you do if this were your prospect? How would you add value in the follow-up?"

PASSIVE FOLLOW-UP

Suppose you have been working with a prospect for a long period of time, but you can feel the sale slipping away. You ascertain that there is a 1 percent chance you'll get the sale six months from now.

Is it worth your time and energy for active follow-up? I don't believe so. This is where your CRM program can really help you out. This is the time for passive follow-up.

By passive I mean that the system will do the follow-up work by way of automated outreach. Your job now is to populate the CRM with solid, useful, and valuable content.

Set up your CRM so that you have a designation for "long-term prospects." I recommend that you have a standing weekly task to send out value-added content.

Over the past decade, content marketing has proven to be an incredibly valuable method of staying connected with potential customers. What does that look like?

- Articles that would appeal to your customer base
- Testimonials from current customers

- Photos (but not too many, and not too high a resolution)
- Product updates and changes
- Events that would be of interest
- Industry insider information

You never know when that content will reach the right prospect at the right time.

FROM THE FIELD

"By chance I kept calling a prospect who never answered his cell. After at least seven attempts by phone I was about to give up. Finally, on the eighth attempt, I come to find out he was traveling with a business phone and had forgotten his cell. He answered, 'Damn, Pete, it's about time. Where you been? Let's do this thing!'"

HOW TO GIVE UP

Alas, you're not going to get them all. At some point you'll need to give up and move on. Here are a few tips to help in different situations.

On that last conversation . . .

Your customer honored you with his time and attention. That deserves a thank you at the least. You honored your customer with helpful information and your valuable time. A small request is not out of order. It might sound something like this:

"It's been a pleasure to help you on this journey. I'm disappointed that we won't be doing business together, but I respect your decision and I still enjoyed the time spent. If you feel that I was helpful, I would deeply appreciate a referral. Is there anyone who comes to mind that might benefit from working with me"?

This works equally well in an email or a handwritten note. Either way, end with a warm thank you.

> *Accept failure as part of the process.*
>
> —UNKNOWN

THE GUT CHECK

You should feel *horrible* if . . .

- You're not 100 percent sure they were going to move on.
- You did not give them your very best efforts.
- You gave up after just a few impersonal contacts.

You should feel *great* if . . .

- You maintained a positive relationship until the end.
- You are in a position to ask for and receive referrals.
- You can say with certainty you did everything you could do.

Self-Study Questions:

1. For the last five customers you've "let go of," what are the reasons you've stopped follow-up? After reading this chapter, which, if any, of these customers should you still try to reach out to?

2. How do you normally break up with cold leads? If you normally just stop calling, is it worth trying the How to Give Up guidelines?

3. Do you have a passive follow-up process? If not, what do you need to do to make that happen?

4. If you were ghosted by someone you were dating, how much follow-up would you keep doing? Why does it make sense that sales follow-up should go on longer?

5. Why is a thank you to a customer for *not* making a purchase and not even being consistent at communicating back to you a good idea in the long run?

Now Do This:

Pick one customer who hasn't given you a clear and compelling reason to shut down follow-up, and reach out again. Find a good reason to call. Make that call!

PART IV
KILLIN' IT

19

The 1 Percent Club

Don't fail one step before success. Go the
extra mile to be part of the 1 Percent Club! You
become a superstar by applying three parts
of a formula: focus, persistence, and time.

THE KNEE OF THE CURVE

Are you familiar with the term "knee of the curve" (see figure)?

The Long-Term Payoff of Consistent Follow-Up

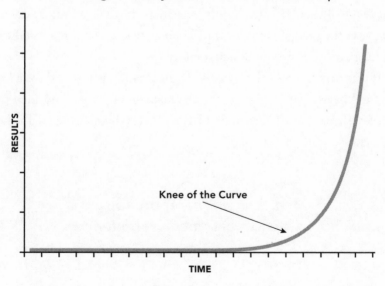

The vertical axis in the graph demonstrates performance levels; the horizontal axis measures time.

The curve represents the long, slow ascent toward success. It is the plodding process of constant improvement and perseverance. There are slow gains at first. In fact, it might feel like there is no improvement at all. But this is about pressing on when you want to give up and perfecting your craft. It's about delayed gratification.

And then . . . *boom!* There is a tipping point that suddenly vaults your performance to sky-high levels. That moment in time is represented graphically as the knee of the curve, that moment when your results suddenly skyrocket.

The Beatles kicked off the so-called British Invasion of the United States in the 1960s, taking the country by storm. Seemingly overnight the Beatles were everywhere. You could not walk down the street without hearing a Beatles song. You could not turn on the television without seeing a Beatles performance. Young people went wild. Old people plugged their ears.

The Beatles were an overnight sensation. And it only took them years upon years of unheralded and grueling work to become so. Few people are even aware of their all-night stints in small, dimly lit clubs in Hamburg, Germany. The group played for endless hours to sparse crowds, but during that long process they found their identity.

If you were to chart the progress of the Beatles, you would see a long, slow, and nearly parallel line along the horizontal plane. And then they recorded *Please Please Me*, their first LP, and everything changed. The knee of the curve.

> *Mediocrity will never do. You are capable of something better.*
>
> —GORDON B. HINCKLEY

How many sales professionals have labored long and hard doing the same things as everyone else, only to find that their success is somehow limited? Where is the knee-of-the-curve moment for sales professionals?

I'll tell you where it is: follow-up! Follow-up is the missing link that vaults mediocre salespeople to extraordinary levels of success.

WHY NOT?

But wait a second, Jeff. If follow-up is the simple answer, why don't more salespeople do it? Why is follow-up the forgotten task?

Because it's not sexy. It's not the part of the process that salespeople enjoy the most. It requires diligence and patience and stamina and discipline. It requires something that is woefully lacking in society today: the acceptance of delayed gratification.

It requires the Big P: Persistence.

Persistence is about staying on the court and practicing your jump shot for an hour after your teammates have gone home. It's about plucking a guitar until your fingers bleed to play one particularly difficult riff perfectly. It's about staying in the crime laboratory and poring over evidence for the eighteenth time, looking for that missing clue that will solve the case.

> ### FROM THE FIELD
>
> "I had clients that I reached out to a minimum of once a month for two years, and they ended up buying a $650,000 house from me. Persistence and just touching base to make them feel important was key."

Top performers do not rest until every performance box has been checked. It's not about doing what is comfortable; it is about doing what is right.

You gotta want it. And you gotta want it pretty bad to stay with it.

> *Athletes train 15 years for 15 seconds of performance. Ask them if they got lucky. Ask an athlete how he feels after a good workout. He will tell you that he feels spent.*
>
> —SHIV KHERA

THE BILL PORTER STORY

You may have seen Bill Porter when he was featured on the ABC show *20/20* back in the 1990s. Or perhaps you caught his story in *Door to Door*, the movie made about his life. Bill Porter was the number-one salesperson in the United States for Watkins Industries, a manufacturer of health remedies, baking products, cleaning supplies, and other household items sold door-to-door by a massive salesforce.

Why all the attention over a door-to-door salesman? Bill Porter had one of the toughest routes in the hilly Portland, Oregon, area, a route he traveled on foot *seven miles a day*, every day. Not easy to do for anyone; much harder if you have cerebral palsy. He slurred his speech. He typed his orders with one finger. He was once hit by a car. And he never, ever, *ever* quit. Bill Porter worked for Watkins Industries as a door-to-door salesman for *40 years*.

Bill Porter became internationally famous—they even made a Japanese movie about his work—but he was no overnight sensation. He hit the knee of the curve after countless grueling hours, days, years.

How much Bill Porter do you have in you? How willing are you to go the extra mile? Scratch that. How willing are you to go the extra *seven* miles?

Being the best of the best doesn't happen because of a wish or a hope or a goal. It is a spot reserved for men and women who take action. And who keep taking action. And who never stop taking action.

> *Sales success comes after you stretch yourself past your limits on a daily basis.*
>
> —OMAR PERIU

MEMBERSHIP IN THE 1 PERCENT CLUB

What is it like to stand in the top 1 percent of your peers? What does it take to find yourself in such an uncrowded space? How does one qualify for the 1 Percent Club?

I'm referring here to the 1 percent of all sales professionals who are truly complete in what they do. Maximum effort and perfected application of skill in *all* areas of the sales process.

The 1 Percenters don't cut corners. They carry extreme amounts of achievement drive; they *have* to win. The 1 Percenters are sickened by the very idea of being like everyone else.

Members of the 1 Percent Club are:

- Driven: They don't rest unless they have given their best effort.
- Methodical: They understand that processes aid in their success planning.
- Focused: They are not easily distracted by what is unimportant. They live in the zone.
- Bold: They lean into their discomforts. They embrace the challenges where others falter.
- Persistent: They don't give up. *Ever.*

Is it hard to get into the club? Yes . . . and no.

You don't simply apply to this club. Desire alone does not give you membership. The entrance fee is years of proven dedication and corresponding results. The club has no interest in "overnight successes." There is no place for those who simply milk a good market.

THE MISSING INGREDIENT

What keeps people out of the 1 Percent Club? You guessed it: a poor record in the area of follow-up. You simply cannot be a complete sales professional without proving your commitment to this critically important discipline.

Put another way, complete success with incomplete effort is not really complete success.

Can follow-up really make that big a difference? I say, emphatically, *yes!* And here's why. Follow-up:

- Separates you from the crowd. You will never be accused of being like every other mediocre salesperson putting in the minimum of effort.

- Grows your confidence. You become bolder and surer of yourself when you know that you are doing what matters.

- Gains attention. People notice when you are pursuing diligent follow-up efforts. Your boss notices, your peers take note, but mostly your customers pay heed.

- Makes you memorable. When it comes to making a final decision, customers will remember you because you gave them very good reasons to do just that.

Follow-up is the one thing that will have the biggest impact on making the 1 Percent Club.

THE COMPOUND EFFECT

When you are finished with this book, I encourage you to read *The Compound Effect*. Darren Hardy's short but powerful instructions will teach you important truths about the power of persistence over time.

The Compound Effect suggests that little things, done properly and over time, will have a huge payout. You may not see instant success, but in the long run your success will grow exponentially.

Follow-up is a perfect example of the Compound Effect.

Follow-up isn't about a program; it's about a habit. It's about doing the right thing, over and over again, day in and day out.

It's about a very long walk, a walk you are still taking when others have dropped out. It takes focus, persistence, and time.

No one accidentally climbs a mountain. No one accidentally builds a home with their own hands. No one accidentally becomes a self-made millionaire. And no one accidentally joins the 1 Percent Club.

Are you in? Prove it. Don't tell me. Show me.

Self-Study Questions:

1. How would better follow-up compound your effectiveness?

2. What are some of the things you're already doing well to be a "complete sales professional"?

3. What is the one biggest change you can make in your follow-up approach to move along the path to be eligible for the 1 Percent Club?

4. How will you continue applying the skills you've learned in earlier chapters to build the follow-up habits you need for greater success?

Now Do This:

The 1 Percent Club has plenty of room for more complete sales professionals. You can be the next 1 Percenter. All it takes is follow-up. It ain't easy, but it's worth it. Now go do it!

20

Beyond 1 Percent

*We perform at our highest level
when we serve others.*

KNOWING VERSUS DOING

I'm grateful you took on something important and worked through your discomfort and reluctance. You were motivated to find success and even enjoyment in the follow-up process. You are making more sales and serving more people. Because, at the end of the day . . .

We perform at our highest level when we serve others.

It's time to take a victory lap, my friends. It is time to reflect on the journey you've undertaken, to celebrate the progress you've made along the way, and to grow your confidence for the next part of your career expedition.

If you've not only *read* the book but you've also *done* the book, you should be seeing marked improvement in your follow-up efforts and the corresponding incremental sales. If you've not taken any implementation steps, now is the time.

> *Good luck is when opportunity meets preparation, while bad luck is when lack of preparation meets reality.*
>
> —Eliyahu Goldratt

WHERE DO YOU GROW FROM HERE?

Short-term efforts can bring short-term success. But we're not interested in short-term success. We are looking for excellence, to be great for the rest of our careers, and our careers are very much long term.

So the question is this: How can you sustain success? The answer: Turn your skills into habits.

> *Excellence is an art won by training and habituation. We do not act rightly because we have virtue or excellence, but we rather have those because we have acted rightly. We are what we repeatedly do. Excellence, then, is not an act but a habit.*
>
> —ARISTOTLE

I want you to have the skills. My sincere hope is that this book has helped you to acquire the abilities necessary for follow-up success. But here's the thing about skills: The use and application of said skills is optional. I can go to a yoga class. I can download a video course. I can hire a private instructor. I can learn every position. But I will only be effective if I actually *do* the yoga.

Habits, on the other hand, are not optional. They are so deeply ingrained into my mental routine that I don't know how *not* to do them!

Think about the healthy habits that define our lives. Eating right, flossing our teeth, reading to our children, praying—we do these regularly because we have engrained them into our soul and psyche. They make us who we are.

And how does one develop a habit? By daily repetition. What can you do—*every single day*—to establish a follow-up habit?

Once you've established that habit, it's all about sustaining the momentum. How do you sustain it? By committing to never breaking the string. Practice your follow-up every single day without fail. It takes commitment, but the payoff is incredible.

FROM THE FIELD

We asked, "What keeps you from doing follow-up?" One of you answered, "You have to do it. Nothing should keep you from doing it."

HERE'S TO YOU

Here's to the Winners.

To those who don't just *want* to win but to those who *have* to win. Those who do what it takes when others drop off.

Here's to the Discomfort Embracers.

To those who recognize that the obstacle *is* the path. Those who lean so far into discomfort that they bust right through to the treasure on the other side.

Here's to the Servants.

To those who recognize that winning is a team sport. Those who understand that we are winners when we help other people to be winners.

Here's to the Abundance Thinkers.

To those who are clearheaded enough to understand that there are storehouses of opportunities awaiting those who honor focus, persistence, and time.

Here's to the 1 Percenters.

Here's to *you!*

Notes

Chapter 1

1. Reuben Yonatan, "56 Sales Statistics You Must Know in 2018 & Beyond," *GETCRM*, February 10, 2018, https://getcrm.com/blog/sales-statistics/.
2. Krysta Williams, "53 Sales Follow Up Statistics," *ZoomInfo Blog*, December 6, 2017, https://blog.zoominfo.com/sales-follow-up-statistics/.
3. "118 Eye-Opening Sales Stats You Need to Know (By Category)," *Spotio*, July 30, 2019, https://spotio.com/blog/sales-statistics/.
4. Krysta Williams, "53 Sales Follow Up Statistics," *ZoomInfo Blog*, December 6, 2017, https://blog.zoominfo.com/sales-follow-up-statistics/.
5. Andrew Davies, "The Sales Hierarchy of Lead Data Needs," *Salesforce Blog*, April 17, 2015, https://www.salesforce.com/blog/2015/04/sales-hierarchy-lead-data-needs-gp.html.

Chapter 3

1. Krysta Williams, "53 Sales Follow Up Statistics," *ZoomInfo Blog*, December 6, 2017, https://blog.zoominfo.com/sales-follow-up-statistics/.
2. Pressfield's follow-up book, *Do the Work*, is even better when it comes to beating down the excuses and embracing the tough but important stuff . . . like follow-up!

Chapter 5

1. Check out my interview with Barry Schwartz on my podcast, *The Buyer's Mind*, available on iTunes, Stitcher, and YouTube.
2. Marie Kondo's landmark book *Spark Joy: An Illustrated Master Class on the Art of Organizing and Tidying Up* is a really powerful illustration of elimination as a life-simplifying strategy.

Chapter 6

1. "UberEATS Has Fastest Delivery According to SeeLevel HX Nationwide Food-On-Demand Study," SeeLevel HX, November 15, 2017, https://www.seelevelhx.com/.

2. Alyssa Trenkamp, "Velocify Research Shows Time of Day Has Minimal Impact on Sales Effectiveness; Consider Quick and Strategic Follow-Up Instead," *Velocify by Ellie Mae*, May 26, 2016, https://www.velocify.com /newsroom/press-release/velocify-research-shows-time-day-minimal-impact -sales-effectiveness-consider-quick-strategic-follow-instead (access date October 31, 2019).
3. James B. Oldroyd, Kristina McElheran, and David Elkington, "The Short Life of Online Sales Leads," *Harvard Business Review*, March 2011, https:// hbr.org/2011/03/the-short-life-of-online-sales-leads (accessed October 29, 2019).
4. "Twenty Experts Answer: What's Your #1 Sales Follow-Up Tip?," Tenfold (sales blog), 2016, https://www.tenfold.com/call-scripts/20-experts-answer -whats-your-1-sales-follow-tip/.

Chapter 9

1. Lisa Furgison McEwen, "How Images Impact Email Campaigns—This May Surprise You," *Pinpointe Marketing Blog*, December 28, 2016, https://www .pinpointe.com/blog/how-images-impact-email-campaigns.

Chapter 10

1. For further study, view stats here: "25 Mobile App Usage Statistics to Know in 2019," *MindSea*, https://mindsea.com/app-stats/ (accessed October 27, 2019).
2. Brian Fung, "Report: Americans got 26.3 Billion Robocalls Last Year, up 46 Percent from 2017," *The Washington Post*, January 29, 2019, https://www .washingtonpost.com/technology/2019/01/29/report-americans-got-billion -robocalls-last-year-up-percent/.

Chapter 11

1. "Email and Spam Data," Cisco Talos Intelligence Group, February 2020, https://talosintelligence.com/reputation_center/email_rep (access date March 4, 2020).
2. Sherman Standberry, "8 Simple Techniques to Improve Your Email Open Rate," *Lyfe Marketing Blog*, September 20, 2019, https://www.lyfemarketing .com/blog/email-open-rate/.
3. "Email Marketing Benchmarks," Mailchimp, October 2019, https:// mailchimp.com/resources/email-marketing-benchmarks/ (accessed October 27, 2019).
4. "Mobile Is Now the Preferred Platform for Reading Email with More Than Half of All Email Opens," Return Path, July 18, 2017, https://returnpath

.com/newsroom/mobile-now-preferred-platform-reading-email-half-email
-opens/.

5. Allen Finn, "35 Face-Melting Email Marketing Stats for 2018," *WordStream*,
   August 26, 2019, https://www.wordstream.com/blog/ws/2017/06/29/email
   -marketing-statistics.

Chapter 12

1. Kenneth Burke, "107 Texting Statistics That Answer All Your Questions,"
   Text Request, May 24, 2016, https://www.textrequest.com/blog/texting
   -statistics-answer-questions/.
2. Aja Frost, "How to Text Sales Prospects (and Double Your Conversion Rate),"
   HubSpot Blog, January 20, 2017, https://blog.hubspot.com/sales/text-sales
   -prospects.
3. "Text Messaging Is Absolutely Eating Phone Call's Lunch," Franchise Help,
   https://www.franchisehelp.com/franchise-lead-generation/more-evidence
   -that-text-messaging-is-eating-phone-calls-lunch/ (accessed October 31,
   2019).
4. Steve Olenski, "Pulling Back the Curtain on Text Message Mobile
   Marketing," *Forbes*, March 4, 2013, https://www.forbes.com/sites
   /marketshare/2013/03/04/pulling-back-the-curtain-on-text-message-mobile
   -marketing/#7d1ff36710d9.
5. "Text Messaging for Better Sales Conversion," *Velocify by Ellie Mae*, http://
   engage.velocify.com/TextMessagingforBetterSalesConversion (accessed
   October 31, 2019). Also available at http://pages.velocify.com/rs/leads360
   /images/Text-Messaging-for-Better-Sales-Conversion.pdf.

Chapter 13

1. Terrance Kwok, "3 Sales Emails Proven to Boost Reply Rates by 8x," Vidyard,
   December 6, 2016, https://www.vidyard.com/blog/3-sales-emails-boost-reply
   -rates/.
2. Kimbe MacMaster, "3 Reasons Video is a Phenomenal Sales Tool,"
   Vidyard, January 18, 2017, https://www.vidyard.com/blog/video-sales-tool
   -infographic/.
3. "Using Personalized Videos in Modern Sales Engagement," SalesLoft, https://
   salesloft.com/resources/blog/using-personalized-videos-in-modern-sales
   -engagement/ (accessed October 30, 2019).
4. "Video Marketing Statistics 2019: The State of Video Marketing 2019,"
   Wyzowl, December 2018, https://www.wyzowl.com/video-marketing
   -statistics-2019/ (accessed October 31, 2019).

5. M. Taylor, "New Research: Twitter Users Love to Watch, Discover and Engage with Video" *Twitter Blog*, May 13, 2015, https://blog.twitter.com /marketing/en_us/a/2015/new-research-twitter-users-love-to-watch-discover -and-engage-with-video.html.

Index

About the Author

Jeff Shore is the founder and president of Shore Consulting, Inc., which specializes in field-tested and proven psychology-based sales training programs. Jeff is a top-selling author, an award-winning keynote speaker, and the host of the popular sales podcast *The Buyer's Mind*.

With over 30 years of real-world, frontline experience, Jeff developed advanced sales strategies from extensive research into the psychology of buying and selling. He teaches salespeople how to climb inside the minds of their customers to sell the way their buyers want to buy. Using these game-changing techniques, Jeff Shore's clients generated over $30 billion in sales last year.

Jeff holds the prestigious Certified Speaking Professional designation from the National Speakers Association and is a member of the NSA's exclusive Million Dollar Speaker's Group. As comfortable with CEOs of Fortune 500 companies as he is with rookie salespeople, Jeff influences and inspires audiences around the world with his trademark brand of humor, empathy, and hardworking sales tactics.

Jeff lives in the idyllic town of Newcastle, California, with his wife, Karen. When he isn't on an airplane or in front of an audience, you'll find him doting on his tribe of granddaughters, serving at his church, or getting some ice time at the local rink where he plays in a competitive hockey league.

Jeff is the author of multiple books, including *Be Bold and Win the Sale*, which features self-assessment tools, hands-on exercises, and case studies showing Jeff's methods in action. *Be Bold and Win the Sale* is an indispensable resource for any sales professional.

For more information, please visit JeffShore.com.

"Jeff Shore shows how to gain the essential confidence that is the first step to a great sales career."

—Neil Rackham, bestselling author of *SPIN Selling*

978-0071829229